IT'S TIME TO

UNLEASH YOUR STRENGTHS

IT WORKS, BUT ONLY 100% OF THE TIME

by Eddie Villa

TABLE OF CONTENTS:

INTRODUCTION

I want you to imagine that we're hanging out in the most comfortable spot in your house, or in your car, or wherever you are having a chill conversation. We're going to have a conversation about strengths, and we're going to talk about what's great about you and what's great about everyone on this planet. I want to help you be who you are, but not in the trite, "just be yourself" kind of way. I want you to be who you are at a higher level, completely unleashed in and through your strengths.

So many of us have been given this advice throughout our whole lives. We've heard it in the movies. We've heard it in music. We've seen people on stage say, "Hey, just be you! Be true to yourself!" Most of us like hearing it!

We're faced with the same question that Syndrome from the Incredibles ® said to Mr. Incredible. "You always say be true to yourself, but you never say which part of yourself to be true to."

I'm here to teach you that you don't have to wear different hats for different parts of your life. You get to be YOU at the highest level in every area of your life from your relationships, to your business, in your health, and in your belief in yourself.

The question is how is that articulated? Imagine going in for a job interview, or out on a first date. Someone asks you, "Tell me about yourself." Can you answer that question without talking about how many kids you have; without talking about what you do for a living; without even talking about physical appearance, skin color, nationality, where you were born, or your religion? Imagine being able to answer that question in a way that is true to who you are, that has nothing to do with any outside variables, in a way that makes you unique, different than anybody who ever has, or will be, on this planet!

That is what this book is about. The reason that I'm doing this is because I want to help all of us embrace who we are.

It's easy to get caught up in who or what we're not. It comes from looking at famous people, leaders, or other people who hold a status that you want to have, or admire. We think to ourselves, "I want what they have, but I guess I can't have it, because I could never do what they do, or be who they are."

Many years ago, I went through this journey from hating myself to unleashing my strengths. I finally realized the secret to life wasn't to just do what the successful people do; it was to do what works for me. Once I figured that out, everything changed. I'll dive deeper into my story later, but I'm hoping to help you love who you are. Once you do, everything lines up- money, better health, better relationships, and a belief in yourself that is unshakeable.

Byron Katie wrote *Loving What Is*, an incredible book that I read a long time ago, which changed my life. Katie talks about three different businesses:

1. Your Business
2. Other People's Business
3. God's Business

What happens is this: when we're in one of these businesses, we are always happy, and we always get what we want. We're doing things in a way that is uplifting, energetic, and has a successful endgame. Unfortunately, when we're in the other two businesses, we are quite the opposite: disconnected, unproductive, and uncreative. Ultimately, we get in other people's way. I want to share the summary of these businesses, as a reference, so you can understand what I'm talking about.

Everything that you think, feel, do, and create, falls under "your business." When you are in your business, you're productive. You love yourself and it's easier to love others. You are focused on your thoughts, feelings and actions instead of trying to control the thoughts, feelings and actions of others.

The second is Other People's Business, which is what? Simple. It's everything they are thinking, feeling, doing, and creating. Whenever we are in other people's business, we are only aware of what they're doing and creating. We lose ourselves. We start creating stories in our head about what they're thinking and feeling. As you can tell, there is no way that we could know what's actually going on in someone else's head, and there's no way that we can really know what they're feeling. So, because we don't know what they're thinking or feeling, the stories in our heads lead us to assumptions about what they are doing and why.

I'm telling you right now, every single time we do that, we end up being angry, frustrated, lonely, depressed, and we become something that we are not. This includes that simple truth that we are NOT those other people. We have to understand that they've created realities in their heads that lead them to do what they're doing. Their realities differ from our own. We can't know what they're thinking or feeling. It's impossible.

Truth is, we do it the most with the people we love the most; the ones that we think we know more than anybody else. Who are these people? Family members, spouses, children; all of these are who we think we know best. But, when we tell our stories about their thoughts and feelings, it's really bad. We end up showing up at our worst; with the people we love the most.

Ultimately, I want you to think about this: how many times have you been upset with your children? You start to think that you know what they're thinking. You know why they did something, even after you told them not to do it. You become inauthentic. You start doing things like I do. Whenever I'm yelling at my kids, or I get frustrated with them, I walk away going "Oh, why did I do that?" "I really wish I didn't have to do it that way, but they made me." We've done that, more than we realize. We do it with our spouses. We do it with our siblings and other family members. We likely did it with our parents. We do it with everybody around us.

What I'm trying to do is help you open up your eyes and see what you are doing, to keep you from becoming something that you're not.

The third and final business is the worst place to be. It's the place where so many of us go so easily: God's Business. Everything else that is outside of us, and outside of other people, becomes God's Business. It's the things we can't control, even when we're there:

the weather, the traffic, how people react in large crowds. We think that good things should only happen to good people, and bad things to bad people. When you see good things happening to bad people, and bad things to good people, you want to play God, and every time you do it, it leads to anger, frustration, loneliness, and depression, which then leads you to be things that are not you. Then what next?

What happens every single time is you end up disconnecting from the people you care about. You end up getting in people's way. You end up becoming uncreative, and unproductive. If you want to be what and who you aren't, inauthentic with everything you do, then get in Other People's Business, and God's Business. My hope is that while you're reading this, you've made the decision that you don't want to do that anymore.

Right now you're looking back at your life and realizing how getting in Other People's and God's Business is preventing you from being yourself at a high level and getting what you want. Think about it harder and you'll realize it happens about 100% of the time. My hope is that you've made the decision to continue reading with complete conviction and commitment to staying in your business and discovering how to be who you are at the highest possible level in everything you do.

I'm going to help you stay in your business with everything you do, and show you how to do it. It's where you are going to be the happiest, most productive, creative, and influential. You'll be able to move communities forward in a positive way. You'll be able to get things done that have been obstacles before, but now you'll do it at the high level that you want. You'll be able to be more creative, and connect with the right people in the world. We're going to do a lot of that, so stick with me for the rest of this book, because it's time to own and love who you are and then Unleash Your Strengths in every aspect of your life.

BEFORE CONTINUING ANSWER THESE QUESTIONS AS BEST AS YOU CAN RIGHT NOW:

WHO ARE YOU?

WHAT DO YOU SAY WHEN SOMEONE ASKS, "TELL ME ABOUT YOURSELF?"

WHAT DO YOU SAY WHEN SOMEONE ASKS, "WHAT DO YOU DO FOR A LIVING?"

WHAT PERCENTAGE OF THE TIME DO YOU RESIDE IN GOD'S OR OTHER PEOPLE'S BUSINESS VS. YOUR OWN?

CHAPTER 1
WHAT HAPPENED

It was March of 2018. I was attending a leadership event for a large network marketing company that my wife and I belong to. We had just hit a distinguished rank in the company and our income was really taking off. We were doing well.

The money that we were making was actually pushing us to work harder because I was seeing how the income was allowing me the opportunity to be of value to others, to do more, to help more people, and that's all I wanted. So, even though we had to hit a high rank, and our income was more money than I'd ever really made in my life, I wasn't willing to coast and rest on my laurels. The success and income was giving me the freedom to help and empower more people.

Two goals came to my mind during the event.

1. I want to move to the next rank: I want to be able to create an even higher residual income, because I could clearly see that I could help more people.

But it had to be done with my second goal in mind.

2. Go to the next level in a way that honors who I am.

I have seen too many people sabotage their success because they don't like who they were becoming in the process of growing an income or business. I wanted to avoid the internal struggle, which is why I needed to honor myself. But the problem was the same issue I mentioned in the introduction. Who am I really?

I knew who I was as a husband, a parent to seven kids, a successful leader, but outside of all those things. I had no idea. If somebody would ask me, "Eddie, who are you?" I would just tell them all the things I accomplished. That was really frustrating because I feared that if I never understood who I was, then I would not be able to know how to increase my success, how to enjoy more success, or how to feel worthy of success. Worthiness was an issue for me, and a lot of people in our business who were experiencing similar levels of success. I didn't want to throw it away because I didn't have an answer to the existential question, "Who am I?"

During this event, I was taught something that made a difference for me. I learned from the company Gallup®. They came into my world at exactly the right time. I took their CliftonStrengths® assessment, which is a tool to help people know what their Strengths are, as Gallup® defines them.

I did the assessment with some level of skepticism. I kept thinking, "How could anybody else know who I am, if I don't know who I am?"

Have you ever had a situation where somebody comes up to you and shares a little bit of information that changes everything for you? That is exactly what happened for me.

They drew a star diagram. I want you to picture a star in your head. What's great about a star is that it has these five high points, right? But, it also has low points in between. So, the analogy was that the high points were my strengths and talents, and the low points were my weaknesses. They showed what happens when you try to develop your weaknesses.

When you develop your weaknesses, you increase the low points, and decrease the high points. You're left with a circle. With the intention to invest your time developing weaknesses, you are going to have to neglect your talents and strengths. One must go up while the others falter. Ultimately, your star becomes a circle.

That was it! My big, light bulb moment. They said, "If we spend time developing our weaknesses, we lose our talents and strengths." How I interpreted that was this: every minute I invest trying to develop a weakness, I am becoming mediocre at best. That was when my brain clicked, and I immediately thought, "Oh, I'm not interested in that. I am not interested in becoming mediocre. I'm not going to work on a weakness, just to become invisible."

I decided that I was never going to develop a weakness again. Instead, I was going to figure out how to be good at everything, by just allowing myself to embrace my strengths, the ones that have been there and helped me in the past. I resolved to focus on that. I truly believed in that moment, that I could have anything I wanted without having to change who I was. I decided it was actually more about changing how I saw myself, embracing myself, and then being myself at the highest possible level.

Everything changed for me at that moment. I had the big epiphany! I realized how I'd been doing life up until that moment and decided I was going to complete integrity with who I am at my core moving forward. I decided to no longer do two things. One: try to improve a weakness. Two: compare myself to others. I was done! Comparing myself to others and focusing on developing my weaknesses, led me to not knowing who I am, which then led me to not loving who I am and embracing it with everything I do.

I want you to go along with me on this journey, because my next step, after that, was to learn everything about strengths. I wanted to know everything that Don Clifton knew. I wanted to know everything that the people on stage knew, and what they didn't know. One of my strengths is called Competition® . I love my Competition® strength because I use it to push me. When I see other people who are good at things, it pushes me to be better.

So, here was my plan: I went on a rampage. I opened up my full 34 strengths report. I looked at the entire detailed report, which I'll come back to later, but I wanted to know everything about my strengths and how they worked. For instance, I wanted to know why my strengths are in the sequence that they are and why the order mattered.

I wanted to know everything about Strengths, but I also wanted to know everything about everyone else's Strengths. So, I remember at this point I had a plan to turn on my computer, go online, and invite everybody I knew, so that I could become a "Strengths Ninja." I was pretty influential at the time, because we were successful in our business, and we had created a name for ourselves: my wife and I. I leveraged that popularity to get people to come to a workshop with me for free, for six weeks. I coached over 150 people for free, but I kept going. For a year and a half I invested my life into coaching people every day until I had coached over 1200 people, for free.

I also went to Gallup®, took their certification course, became a Certified Strengths Coach, and then kept moving forward. The learning was more massive. I learned things about strengths at such a fast pace that I started to know things that the average strength coach doesn't know. I will cover them all throughout this book, which contains everything I know about strengths that Gallup® does or doesn't talk about. I want to share all of this value with you. For me, it was really about getting to know strengths at a deeper level.

Now, there was a big problem. I was doing this for free for a year and a half, and I'll tell you right now, my wife did not like this at all. She kept reminding me that we got into the business so that we could have free time and do whatever we wanted.

What she didn't realize was that this is what I wanted to do with my free time. I wanted to coach people to understand their strengths, and themselves, at a deeper level. I am so grateful that she was patient, although she didn't understand what I was really doing. I'm grateful for that time because I was not only learning things that Gallup® didn't talk about, but more importantly, the things I was learning were actually making an impact. I was making an impact with so many people that eventually, word started to get around about what I was really doing, and how I was really helping people.

As word grew, it got really popular. People started listening to me. At any point in time, I could do a free webinar or training and have between 300-600 people join the call. What I was doing was building a list of people who would be interested in doing what I was going to do next, but there was another roadblock. This is where it got really weird. I got so good at understanding people's strengths through their reports that I started to see aspects about them that were very personal. For instance, about 50 people sent me their strengths reports, and these were not just regular people.

These were people who made between six and seven figures a year in the network marketing business.

I was looking at people who were the top notch, one percentile of the company. They were sending me their strengths reports and it started getting really weird. After about five minutes I started to know them intimately, so then I would start recording on my phone for about 30 minutes, breaking down each person's strengths, and sending it back to them. My friends, I was going on and on about people I had never met, but I loved what I was doing so much that I just kept doing it and never stopped.

I would send these videos back to these total strangers who trusted me with their strengths reports, and I was sharing intimate details about them: not just what's great about them, but I was seeing how their life was in conflict in certain areas. I was even seeing certain people who had traumatic pasts. I was noticing where certain people struggle in their marriages or their relationships, or their business, or their health. I was unveiling so many things that were deep and intimate, that they would message me back saying things like, "Eddie, you have no idea what you've done!" The feedback I was getting from these videos was astounding. Some people were flat out crying because of what I was telling them. Some people's coaches were reaching out to me, surprised because they had been trying to work through these triggers for months and I was cracking them in 30 minutes.

The coaches would ask, "How could you possibly know all of that from their about strengths report?" The detail at which I was seeing a person through their report was awesome at first, but then it got creepy, really creepy. I started to think that I shouldn't be doing this because I didn't want to come across as a fortune teller looking at people through a crystal ball. Now, look, I have nothing against people who read tarot cards or do palm readings, but it's not exactly the way I wanted to see strengths. I didn't want that stigma of something that wasn't really me.

By this time, I had invested over a year and a half of my life into understanding strengths reports. I was getting weirded out by what I was able to see in people. I almost threw it all away. I remember having a conversation with God where I said, "I'm not doing this anymore." Then I told my wife Angela that I was not going to be the "strengths guy." But the next two days created a powerful moment in my life. During that prayer period, all I could think about was strengths reports, and not being the "strengths guy." It was all that my mind wanted to process. I wanted to look at more reports, and learn more. Every time I looked at a new report, it was something different, and I started realizing that I wasn't just learning about all of these people. I was also learning about myself.

So, after two days of declaring, "I'm not the Strengths Guy," I finally gave in and had another conversation with God that went something like this, "All right, fine, God. If this is what you want me to do, I have to go all in here. I can't do it halfway. I'm going to get crazy obsessed with this whole process in a way that I'm about to take it to a whole new level. Please, God, please don't make it hard on me."

I remember saying that, and deciding to move ahead with it. I decided to open up a private group and I pushed, and I made it a big deal. It was at this exact moment that I realized that by being who I am, not only could I find truth and add value for myself, but I could make it very easy for other people to see their value as well. So easy, in fact, that the owner of the largest network marketing company in the United States, and also the largest essential oil company in the world, came to me and personally said, "Eddie, what you are doing with strengths is beyond what Gallup® is doing. You have found your calling. Keep going! We need this right now!" So, my friends, when God himself plus a high profile business leader told me to keep going, there was nothing that was going to stop me.

I dove in even further, and in the year and a half since those conversations, and since that process, I have generated a multiple six figure income from owning and applying who I am to help other people do the same. I've also figured out ways to improve my already successful marriage and my ability to parent my children, which is now all about using my strengths. I've learned about improving my health, my finances, and my leadership abilities.

I want you to have these experiences. I want you to have your own process of loving and embracing who you are and then learning how to be yourself at an even higher level.

This book is here to help you. It is for you whether you want to be a better leader at work, or in your home, be a better spouse, a better parent, or whatever. Even if you're already a high level executive, but maybe you struggle with having people in your organization follow your energy, this is for you. Maybe you struggle with helping other people find their own power and strength because you noticed that they're leaning on you a little too hard. Or, maybe, like everyone else, you're sick and tired of comparing yourself to others. Ultimately, this book is for anybody who wants to learn how to do everything in a way that embraces who they are, so they can stop trying to be something they're not. So, let's get into how your strengths report works to help you be you.

QUESTIONS:

WHAT ARE YOUR 'WEAKNESSES'?

WHAT HAVE YOU BEEN TOLD YOU NEED TO DEVELOP?

IF YOU WERE FORCED TO ANSWER THE QUESTION "WHAT IS YOUR CALLING IN LIFE?" WHAT WOULD YOU SAY?

CHAPTER 2
WHY YOU ARE AWESOME

Whenever I look at a person's report, I don't think about strengths and I don't think about Don Clifton, and I certainly don't think about Gallup®. I think about you, and why you are so awesome. In this chapter, I'm going to share how your strengths report proves you are amazing.

I'm often asked, "Eddie, what's so great about this strengths stuff?" I give them an answer that immediately makes them go out and pay to get their full 34 strengths report.

First thing I want you to do is think about how many people are on the planet, which is about 7.7 billion people. Now, when you take this assessment, there are odds, or chances, that another person could possibly have the same report as you. I want you to be aware of this, because I hate personality tests. I have always hated them, because their purpose is to put you in a group, and I don't feel like I belong to any one group exclusively. So, if I don't belong in a group, then how could a personality test help me understand who I am?

The strengths assessment is different. It helps you understand how you fit into any group that you want, but also helps you understand your differences with everyone. I'll tell you that through these odds, the chances of any one person having the same results as you goes something like this.

If every person, 7.7 billion people, got their results, the chances of having the same top five, in a different order, as others would be 1 in 280,000. Breaking the math down from 7.7 billion and dividing it by 280,000, that would be roughly 27,500 people on earth that have the same top 5 strengths as you.

However, the order does matter, because the odds that someone would have the same top 5, in the same order, would be 1 in 33 million. In the entire world, there are 234 people who have the same top 5 in the same order. Imagine that! You started off in an arena or stadium with 27,500 people, and more than 99% of those people left, and you are left with just 234 people who have the same top 5 in the same order.

Let's move further. If we add the sixth strength, out of your full 34, the chances of another person having the same top six becomes just under 1 in 1 billion. You are now in a room with seven or eight people. Once we move to the seventh strength, the chances of having the same order are incredibly low. Just from your top seven, you are different from anybody else. Now we're really talking.

Guess what? The chance of any person having the same 34 strengths in the same order as you is more than one in 131 billion. Why does 1 in 131 billion matter? That happens to be the estimate of how many people have lived on the planet all the way through 2050, which is 30 years from now.

The big takeaway is that you, me, and everybody else on this planet is infinitely unique and cannot be duplicated. You are someone that has never been, nor ever will be on this planet. What you have to offer, nobody else can. That means that when you are being you at a high level, you bring something that nobody else can. When you doubt yourself, nobody gets to experience you. Nobody gets that value, especially you, and that is the biggest travesty of this whole thing. Ultimately, when people think that who they are is not unique, or they think that they are common, then what we all do is deny ourselves, and the rest of the world, the one thing that we are destined to give: add value to others.

Think about all of the people you've compared yourself to. You've done it. Maybe you compare yourselves to other moms on Instagram, or maybe you're a dad who doesn't feel like he fits in with other dads, or a business leader who sees others being more fruitful and successful. Maybe you're a competitive athlete, or maybe you're a normal person who has looked at others and said to yourself, "I can't be good like them," and that has shut down your mindset.

Those people are also infinitely unique and cannot be duplicated! That means that you cannot be them. You're not supposed to. They can't be you, and they aren't supposed to either. What I've learned in my years of working with a lot of people, especially very high income people, is that the people who have the most happiness and success in their lives are the ones who figured out how to embrace who they are better than others.

My friends, the only person you should ever compare yourself to is you, because you're the only one that you can actually be. That should light you up right now and make you realize that there's no one else to compare yourself to. All you have to do is figure out who you are and be that with everything you do, being infinitely unique. That means you must embrace who you are in order to find that happiness that you really want. It's time to help you identify those keys by looking at your strengths report.

QUESTIONS:

WHAT DOES IT MEAN TO KNOW YOU ARE INFINITELY UNIQUE
AND CANNOT BE DUPLICATED?

WHAT WOULD YOU DO TODAY KNOWING THAT YOU ARE
PERHAPS THE ONLY ONE ON EARTH CAPABLE OF DOING IT?

CHAPTER 3
THE DOMAINS: THE SOLUTION
FOR HESITATION

Gallup® took the 34 strengths and unique talents that they talk about, and they grouped them into four domains. These domains ended up being this big magic secret that helped me help other people recognize and understand their own report at a very high level, very quickly.

Most people, after taking their assessment, look at their top five, or their full 34, and try to decipher what it all means. How do they work and apply it? When I started to understand how the domains work, I started to see how it helped other people get through the confusion when it comes to strengths and help them take immediate steps to get success. There's a secret code, a combination, a hack, if you will, a way to apply your strengths and understand them by putting them immediately into action, instead of having to go on a retreat to learn.

How many times have you ever been tempted to go on a weeklong retreat in the middle of nowhere; where they dump you in the desert at night and you get chased by wolves? You know what I'm talking about. I'm sure there is a retreat out there like this, just so that you can find out who you are in your heart, right? Well, without having to do that, we can take the Gallup® strengths assessment and apply what I'm going to teach you about the domains. This is where the magic is.

There's one thing we need to cover before we go into the domains that we need to cover now: hesitation. Somewhere between where you currently are, and where you want to be, is a series of actions that must be taken.

We just have to take action on those steps. We study and learn the steps. We hire coaches, or people who have done it before, to tell us what those things are, then we do it. But there's an elephant in the room: hesitation.

Let me give you an example based on a scenario that has probably happened to you observing hesitation in someone else. How many times have you looked at a person who tells you they want something, but they're not getting it? They're not doing what they need to do to get it. It's tempting to write them off by calling them lazy, or uncommitted.

You gave them labels because you didn't understand the basic concept that's causing them to hesitate. Maybe they really do want those things, and maybe those things really are important to them. Maybe they're not lazy at all, but they haven't figured out the reason for their hesitation. My friends, hesitation is the biggest problem we face on our journey towards getting what we want.

Now, let me explain how people think hesitation works. Let's say the number one represents your starting point and number 10 is where you want to be. Well, you move to points two, three, or four and then a block occurs. Maybe you get tired or burned out or you start doubting yourself. Maybe there's a thought that if you keep pursuing this thing that you want, it'll sacrifice other important priorities in your life. So you stop.

We think that if we just take time off, lower our expectations of ourselves, scroll on Facebook, or do things that help us ignore or dull the pain, then we'll be able to pick back up where we were, right at number 4. What actually happens when we are hesitant is we roll backwards. See, if you work really hard for a couple of months in your business or your life, relationships, health, and then take a break, you actually start to exponentially undo all of the hard work you did to get you where you are. The longer you hesitate, the worse it gets. It's the hesitation that causes the real problem.

What I've learned in working with thousands of people is that hesitation comes when there's something we know we need to do, but we truly believe we can't do it by just being who we are. That's it. It comes from us doubting ourselves. It comes from us believing that we can't keep going authentically. We stop ourselves because we're worried that we have to become something that we are not, in order to progress.

So, we take a break and we step back, sometimes for a day, sometimes for a couple of days, sometimes for weeks, or if you're like me, three and a half years. I spent three and a half years struggling with hesitation because I had worked really hard to move up in a massive corporation, getting promotion after promotion, until one day it all stopped. I hesitated. I changed. I got fired and then for the next few years blamed and berated myself for my failures.

Some hesitation comes from traumatic experiences in our life. When you go through trauma there's a certain level of self-blame that happens, and that self-blame happens because you think you're supposed to have been in control the whole time. Whenever something bad happens, you are frustrated because you look back and you believe you were actually in control when the truth is, you weren't. When you've had a traumatic experience and you blame yourself, then embracing who you are becomes the hardest thing in the world, even though it is the only answer you see. So, you hesitate.

For me, I hesitated for three and a half years during which I worked hard to prove that I was of no value. I worked hard to prove that I was the problem, and there's no way that I could be the solution. Again, my friends, the reason why I understand hesitation is because I've gone through it and worked with so many other people through their own hesitations as well. I mean, these people who make multiple six or seven figures a year, they hesitate, and it blows me away. When I realize that so many of us compare ourselves to people who are just like us, and who struggle, and we think other people are perfect when they're not.

The four domains become the solution to this hesitation problem.

The four domains are:
1. Relationship Building
2. Influencing
3. Executing
4. Strategic Thinking.

Gallup® picked these four domains to represent certain qualities that the strengths share with one another. You can pinpoint your hesitations by reviewing your top 10 strengths. At the same time, these top ten also give you a roadmap to break out of feeling stuck. Each of these domains has their own unique desires, and your report shows you which ones are more important to you.

If you want to do things linearly, from 1 (your starting point) to 10 (where you want to be), you must do everything in a way that honors these unique desires so that you stop hesitating. If you hesitate less, would you be able to finally accept that the success that you've acquired is due to you just being you? It's awesome for me, because I needed something that showed me who I was and these domains made all the difference in the world. So, I'm going to teach you as you review your own strengths report.

Your top 10 strengths are where your energy is highest. Your top 10 strengths represent all the different traits that energize you, that fire you up, that make you inspiring, likeable, or valuable and useful to others.

Your top 10 strengths DO NOT indicate what you CANNOT do. Nope. Get that out of your head right away.

Your strengths report has nothing to do with what you can or cannot do. It shows how you do everything your way, and it works, but only 100% of the time.

This is the golden rule of strengths. I want you to write this down and post it everywhere so you can remember it. Put it somewhere you can see and remind yourself on a daily basis. A lot of people like to look at their strengths report to find proof that they're not good at something or unable to do something. I'm telling you right now, you're not going to find that in the strengths report. This report only shows you the golden rule.

I'm going to repeat it one more time. Your strengths have nothing to do with what you can or cannot do. Your strengths report shows how you do everything your way, and it works, but only 100% of the time.

I want you to see your top 10 strengths as being your zone of genius, as Gay Hendricks put in his book *The Big Leap*. "Your zone of genius is where you are most influential." It's where you are most creative. It's where you are most productive, and it's where you connect with the right people. That's your top 10 strengths. They are right there, in your sequence. Your bottom strengths, which we are going to get into massive detail later, are where you go to do the opposite.

When you doubt who you are and hesitate, and you start rolling backwards, you become those bottom strengths, which puts you in a place where you get in people's way. It's where you become boring and uninteresting. It's where you get lost on social media. It's also where you become unproductive and you start doing things that aren't helping you get what you truly want, and worse, it's where you go to disconnect from others and disconnect from the world, and ultimately, disconnect from you.

Those bottom five strengths are where all the opposites happen. I need you to understand those two dynamics, because your top 10 is where we are going to find your dominant domain and we are going to see what it is that you care about most and what must be honored with everything you do, so you will stop hesitating.

I'm going to break down each of the domains in their own chapter, because there is so much to learn. Before that, all I want you to do is count. A kindergarten child can do this. Count the blues. Count the oranges. Count the purples. Count the greens (or reds if it's an older report). You look at your top 10 strengths and count how many of the ten are relationship building strengths (blue), how many are influencing (orange), executing (purple), and how many are strategic thinking (green or red). Take a look at how many you have of each of these in your top 10 and make a note of it. OK?

I'm going to show you how to understand what this counting exercise demonstrates about you in the next chapters. Suffice it to say, if you have three or more strengths of any domain in your top 10, those represent your dominant domain strengths.

Simply put, these are the ones that represent what must be honored with everything you do going forward. It's really simple. As we go and break down each of these domains in the next chapters, I want you to think about only the ones you have three or more of in the top 10, that's it. If you see a chapter on a domain you don't have three or more of, review it for informational purposes. As you review it, you can better understand other people, and you can help others understand themselves. One last thing before we do this is recall the purpose of these four domains: they are for you to declare who you are, and how you must do everything in a way to stop hesitating.

QUESTIONS:

WHERE HAVE YOU BEEN HESITATING?

HOW IS THE HESITATION AFFECTING YOUR RELATIONSHIPS, HEALTH, BANK ACCOUNT AND BELIEF IN YOURSELF?

HOW MANY STRENGTHS DO YOU HAVE IN EACH DOMAIN IN YOUR TOP 10?

     STRATEGIC THINKING _____
     EXECUTING _____
     RELATIONSHIP BUILDING _____
     INFLUENCING _____

CHAPTER 4
THE RELATIONSHIP BUILDERS
"CONNECT WITH THE RIGHT PEOPLE"

It is my intention during this chapter for me to open up my heart about everything I know when it comes to all of the people I've ever worked with, who have three or more of the relationship building strengths in their top 10. Now, as I go through this, I want you to recognize that even if you have three or more of the relationship building strengths in your top 10, you might also have three or more of another domain, which means, what I share will apply to a lot of your motivations, but not all of them. Just keep that in mind.

What is the dominant desire of a Relationship Builder? If you have three or more relationship building strengths in your top 10, then everything you do must honor a desire for connection. If you're asked to do anything or you believe you need to do something that internally may violate or put this desire at risk, you will hesitate.

The first thing I want to teach you is the dominant desire statement. People who have three or more relationship building strengths in their top 10 have this desire: Connect with the "right people."

Take note of the quotations around "right people," because this can have a very wide open meaning that I've left subjective on purpose. I am not the one to determine who the right people are for you. People message me asking, "Who are the right people? Tell me who the right people are." My answer to them as always, "You tell me who the right people are for you." Now, if you have three or more of the relationship building strengths in your top 10, then connecting has its own meaning, and what connecting means is listening, feeling, and being present, right? Especially if you have strengths like Adaptability®, Includer®, Positivity®, or Harmony®. These strengths really mean to connect with a person without having any kind of outside agenda.

Ultimately, the "right people" can be anybody. There are a couple of strengths I love to talk about that'll really help you identify who the right people are for you. Now, these are extreme examples, so you may fall somewhere in the middle of these. The first one is Relator®. The second one is Includer®. If you have Relator® in your top 10 and you have Includer® in your bottom seven, eight, or nine, it means that the right people for you may be just a few people, and that's really it.

High Relators need to connect with people on a deep level. That means minimal small talk, especially in large groups or at parties. They only want to connect with their people on a profound level, which means it may only be two or three people. So, again, if you have Relator® high and Includer® low, that means you have maybe just a small handful of really deep relationships. What's really awesome about these deep relationships, is these people are the kind of people you can call at 3 am and say "Look, I don't have time to explain, but I need you at my house right now. Please come." Click. You can hang up that phone and you can guarantee that those people would be at your house in a heartbeat without any explanation.

That is amazing. When you are a high Relator, low Includer, you can do that. You can create those deep, meaningful relationships, and the reason why you do that is because you demand such a deep connection with the right people. People that are high Relators and low Includers are the most advanced form of a Relationship Builder that is out there. They like to keep their circle small. These are the kinds of people that if you were to take to a party, (well, let's be honest …. DRAG to a party) the first thing on that person's mind would be, "I'm hoping that there's someone at this party that I know very well. Please let there be someone at this party that I know very well." If you are a high Relator, low Includer, and you can't find a person like that at the party, then your next question is, "is there a pet or a dog or a baby that I can hold, or some plants I could sit next to and connect with?" If they can't find a dog or cat or a baby to hold, then their next thought involves finding a trap door or window through which to escape. Once outside, you might find yourself waiting in the car.

High Relators, low Includers want to avoid or skip boring, small talk conversation as much as possible. These are the kinds of people who get in an elevator praying there's no one in there. As soon as they get in, they hit the close button as fast as they can. They just want to ride that elevator by themselves, because Relators crave deep conversations and deep connections. They are so good at creating those deep connections that they don't do it very often because people have to work really hard to earn their trust. Once you can earn the trust of a high Relator, low includer, you have got someone who's a loyal friend to you forever, and that's massively valuable! People with high Relator, low Includer, are the kind of people that can really make a difference in our lives because they will sacrifice everything for you. I know, because I'm married to one, and I guarantee my mother was also one. High Relators, low Includers are some of my favorite people on the planet.

On the opposite end is the high Includer/low Relator. This is someone who has Includer® in their top 10 and Relator® somewhere between 26 and 34. Essentially a high Includer, low Relator person is open to talk to anyone, anywhere, anytime, for any reason. If they are around people, they are happy. A lot of times, high Includers are so good at being around people that they kind of shape and mold themselves to any situation or conversation because they just want to be around people.

They're also very good at giving people second chances. When other people make mistakes or drop the ball, or even if they fail to deliver on a promise, high Includers are very forgiving. They love to give everyone a second or third or fourth or fifth chance. They want to give them all the extra chances because you never know, people might come around. They might grow and realize they made a mistake and say, "I'm sorry," and come back.

Let's be honest, high Includers are the most prone to give people another nine or ten chances, because who knows, maybe they'll find Jesus. The Includer wants to give everybody an extra chance because they want to make sure that everybody feels listened to, heard, honored, respected, no matter who they are, what their political views are, what the color of their skin is, or what they do for a living. Even if they do horrible things, we can at least give them a chance to wise up and realize they've screwed up. The high Includer will always be there to say, "See, I believed in you the whole time."

High Includers, low Relators are very good at giving people chances, but not as adept at discerning who should or shouldn't be in their circles. They may bring in the wrong people until somebody, somehow, some way, convinces them that they shouldn't have done that. Eventually, they start to make some adjustments. Ultimately, the high Includer, low Relator believes the right people to be connected with could be just about anybody; anybody who just wants to be heard, or involved, will be welcomed by a high includer. They are also very good at recognizing when a certain person is being left out, or when someone is leaving themselves out of the group. The high Includer wants to let them know it's OK to come back in. "You're welcome here." Sometimes the high Includer will also stick up for those that are being left out and speak up for the inclusion of just about anyone.

I frequently get asked, "what if I have both of those strengths high?" or "What does it mean if I have both of them low?" Well let me just sum it up:

High Relator/Low Includer: Prefers to Deepen Relationships with Fewer People

High Includer/Low Relator: Prefers Relationships with Lots of People

High Relator/High Includer: Loves to Deepen Relationships with Lots of People

Middle or Low Includer/Middle or Low Relator: Will connect with people in a way that honors their other dominant domains and strengths.

Wherever these two strengths land will help you determine who your right people are. The important thing is to recognize that your circle of "right people" will be different and distinct from other people. High Includers will expand that circle. High Relators will shrink that circle. Ultimately, in a world where we have the opportunity to connect with many people through social media, we get to decide who our "right people" are by honoring our relationship building strengths.

If you have three or more relationship building strengths in your top 10, if there's anything you have to do that you feel will put relationships at risk, you will hesitate, even if you don't know why. Sometimes you'll tell yourself stories like, "maybe I'm afraid, maybe I don't want it bad enough, or maybe I'm just not good enough for this," and you'll hesitate without realizing the problem. Sometimes you will put your other ambitions on hold because you saw something that you thought would put you at risk of hurting other people or coming off as inauthentic.

This is especially true among Relationship Builders in business or in sales. They're worried that by pushing a product on other people, they're putting their relationship at risk. Even with total strangers, they want to make sure that everything they do is authentic, so they like to say, "I want it to happen organically," instead of forcing it. Relationship Builders want to be in the presence of and in connection with others. If they are asked to do something they feel will risk it, they will stop.

If you have three or more relationship strengths in your top 10, reflect on how nearly every aspect of your life: your health, your relationships, your belief in yourself, your business, your community work, or your job have been more joyful and successful when you are surrounded by and connected with the right people. It's really that simple! If you're being asked to do things that you feel are putting those relationships at risk, then start to communicate that to the people around you. "Hey, I don't want to do this because I'm worried it's going to risk my connection with this person." That person will then start looking for ways to honor that connection.

When you do things to connect with others, you are best when it doesn't include an agenda. I know that's hard for a lot of people to understand, but for the Relationship Builder, you'll notice that your agenda or your ability or what it is you want to do for other people becomes so clear after you've made the connection.

So if you have three or more relationship building strengths in your top ten, you get to make a statement, a public declaration about what's awesome about you. You love to do everything in a way that honors your desire to connect with the right people.

QUESTIONS

HOW MANY RELATIONSHIP BUILDING STRENGTHS DO YOU HAVE IN YOUR TOP 10? WHICH ONES?

WHERE ARE RELATOR® AND INCLUDER® IN YOUR REPORT?

DO YOU PREFER A SMALL CIRCLE OR A LARGER CIRCLE OF CONNECTIONS?

CHAPTER 5
THE INFLUENCING STRENGTHS
"MOVE PEOPLE FORWARD"

If you have three or more Influencing strengths, this chapter is your breakdown. I'm going to talk about what must be honored with everything you do. I'm going to talk about where you really shine, but I'm also going to get in depth about where you drop the ball. I have five influencing strengths, so I understand this one really well. So, buckle up! We're going to have some fun. If you have three or more influencing strengths in your top 10, then the desire that you must honor with everything you do is to **move people forward**.

You must do everything in a way that honors your desire to move people forward. What does "move people forward" mean? It means that you're really good at seeing where people are, especially when you meet a stranger. Whether it's their health, their relationships, their business, or belief in self, you like to make that assessment very quickly, and then you take it a step further and you start to see beyond where they are, to where they could be, and how they can get there. You do this because you're constantly assessing where you are and where you want to be.

The desire to move yourself forward fuels a natural desire to move other people forward with you. You're able to map out, step-by-step, how other people can get to where we all want to be. You see where they can go, and how to get there, but most importantly, the key with Influencers, is that they want to be involved in the process. You want to be in the mix. It's not good enough to hear about other people growing and moving forward, and getting past personal blocks or fears. You want to be in the thick of it, so you can feel like you contributed, or you were part of it in some way.

If you have strengths like Command®, Communication®, Self-Assurance®, or Significance®, these strengths are very intense in the desire to move people forward. You just want to tell people, but that's where you drop the ball. You get excited and wrapped up in what they can do and how they can get there that you actually think it's real. Because you think it's real, you feel like if you don't tell them, something bad is going to happen, so you just come out and tell them, "Oh my gosh, you can do this and this, and here's how to do it. Here's what I do, and this is how I can help you, and you should do it right now." Meanwhile, they just look at you like, "I just met you. That's great. I'm just going to go over there, away from you."

There's a tendency to dump all that information on people without their permission. The dominant influencing domain is so powerful because we get these visions in our head about the people that we meet. We want to see them move. We feel like every minute they're not doing something is wasting that opportunity. You think, "What a travesty, what a terrible thing, if they never fulfill the potential that I see for them." Then you end up doing things that are completely inauthentic to who you are.

You start pushing and demanding, and even pulling them up and dragging them across the finish line. With this comes a level of resentment. Even if they are successful with you pushing or dragging them, there's always resentment, and it creates problems. You see, the dominant Influencer is more interested in seeing other people move forward than having that person like them. This is what I love about dominant Influencers. They care more about you moving forward and reaching your goals than about your opinion of them. That's pretty awesome, but it's powerful and it doesn't need to be controlled; it just needs to be understood.

The dominant Influencers are so good at seeing themselves beyond where they currently are. Where Influencers really struggle is because they see people further along than where those people see themselves. This is especially true if you have Maximizer® high. You always see what's great about the people around you, and then you can see that person beyond that greatness. That's like the difference between a four and a half and a five star hotel. If you've ever stayed in a four and a half star hotel, you know they're really nice, but a Maximizer can see those tiny details that are missing that would make the hotel a five star.

Imagine you're married to a Maximizer, like me, and you notice that the Maximizer is a little hard to impress. It's because they see the greatness in you and only want to see you reach it and achieve it. No matter what you do, even if it's the greatest thing: curing cancer, or changing the world, the Maximizer will continue to see how you can do it better.

The dominant Influencer is always setting the bar beyond where you are and where they see you. Influencers often get disappointed whenever they ask people what they see for themselves, because what that person sees for themselves is so far below what the Influencer sees. The Influencer is let down by that because, in their head, they think that the other person should see beyond that. You will always see them beyond that. Even if a high Influencer meets a person who makes a million dollars a year, they will always think about how they could be making three million a year, just because it's more. Always. You're always seeing people beyond where they see themselves.

Where the Influencer can really make a shift is to stop looking at a person and being disappointed by the fact that their vision is not the same as yours. All you have to do as the Influencer is ask yourself if the vision they have for themselves is on the way towards what you see. If it is, then celebrate it, and be excited because then all you have to do is help them get to where they see themselves, as fast as possible, so that they will then see what you have seen from the start.

Let's put it in mathematical terms. If you meet a person and both of you agree that they are at level one and you see them at level ten, but they only see level five, be grateful that they see level five, and get them to level five as soon as possible, so that they see that it's possible to get to level six, and then level seven. It will keep growing until they get to level ten, which is what you've seen all along. The best way to do this for an Influencer is to just let go of what you visualize for other people and help them visualize what they see in themselves. Help them get closer and closer to what you've seen all along the way. You never have to feel bad about the fact that they don't see what you see.

Most importantly, they never have to feel like they're not good enough for you. The best way to drive someone away or influence them to move backwards, is to make them feel like they're never going to be good enough.

Influencers are so much better when they ask people to articulate where they see themselves and what they want in one year, five years or ten. Be ready to love it no matter what their answer is. Be ready to embrace it, be ready to cheer them on and agree with them. When they say they see themselves in a certain place, ask them how you can help. If you're in the business of helping people make more money and someone asked you to help them make $1,000 a week instead of $500 a week you'll be ready to jump at the opportunity. You can be who you are at a high level, because now they've given you permission. It's a lot more productive. If you are a dominant Influencer, stop putting your visions of what you see of other people onto them without their permission. Instead, get excited about what they see for themselves.

It's important to understand the difference between an Influencer and a Relationship Builder. An Influencer **needs** to see people move forward, and **enjoys** connection. A Relationship Builder **needs** to connect with people, and **enjoys** seeing people move forward. Both of you will risk one over the other. Every time.

One of the things I see a lot is that Relationship Builders will withhold information that will help other people move forward if they feel like releasing that information will put the relationship at risk. If you're a dominant Relationship Builder and you just found out a friend of yours is lying to another friend of yours, can you see how that would put pressure on you to not say anything out of fear that it's going to put your relationship to both of these people at risk? There's hesitancy there. You might do the right thing in the end, but do you feel the resistance, the hesitancy? Influencers have the same thing, when it comes to risking another person moving forward, they will keep information from people out of risk that'll prevent them from moving forward. So, sometimes an Influencer will lie to people out of concern that the information will prevent them from moving forward.

If you have influencing or relationship building strengths in your top 10 you're feeling the real dilemma, the real problem is hesitation. So, instead, as an Influencer, you can go to people and say, "Look, my intention is to help you move forward. I'm more worried about that than I am our relationship. I want you to know that I care more about you getting what you want than your opinion of me. That's the value I bring to you as a friend or as a support."

Influencers, you get to connect with people that want to move forward, then help them make it happen. Get a sense for what those people want, if they want your help, and if they're willing to take the next steps. There's no need to pussy foot around as an Influencer. Put your strengths out there to the forefront, and watch the right people march into your life who want your influence, and watch the wrong people march out or step aside.

QUESTIONS:

HOW MANY INFLUENCING STRENGTHS DO YOU HAVE IN YOUR TOP 10?

IF YOU HAVE MORE THAN THREE, HOW DOES THIS CHAPTER RESONATE WITH YOU?

IF YOU DON'T HAVE MANY INFLUENCING STRENGTHS, WHO DO YOU KNOW WHO SEEMS TO BE A HIGH INFLUENCER? HOW DOES THIS HELP YOU UNDERSTAND THEM?

CHAPTER 6
EXECUTING STRENGTHS
"MAKE SURE THINGS ARE DONE THE RIGHT WAY"

The Executing Domain is one of my favorites because it is so…. not….me. It is, however, my wife, so a lot of what I'm going to be sharing about the executing strengths comes from many years of being married to one of the most amazing people on the planet. I love my wife very much, but I also love picking on her a little bit. This chapter of executing is all about what I've learned.

If you have three or more executing strengths in your top 10, I'm just going to give you some credit right now for getting this far in the book, because dominant Executors really hate being unproductive. They feel like this "head stuff," this nonsense about feelings and hesitation and desires is a big waste of time.

A lot of the Executors would have preferred that I just tell them what to do step by step. The main desire of any dominant Executor is to make sure things are done... the right way. Now, I put a little pause in there on purpose, because if you have Belief® as one of your top executing strengths in your 10, then you probably rejected that right off, and I know you did, and that's okay. I'm going to get into the Belief® strength heavily, pretty soon, because to me, I think it's one of the most important when it comes to teaching people about strengths. So, if you have three or more executing strengths in your top 10, and Belief® is one of them, don't worry.

I already know you don't buy into any of this. You're just reading to see if, maybe, something in here is going to help you be a little bit more productive. The desire of a dominant Executor is to get things done the right way. What is the right way? I know you're all asking this, especially if you have high belief. The right way is any way that you feel is the best way. It can be fast with no thought, or slow with a lot of thoughts. It can be how other people operate best or how you operate best. It can be how you've seen others do it, or how you personally like to do it. The bottom line is productivity.

If you have Deliberative® as one of your top 10 strengths, then thinking things through and logically weighing the pros and cons is important for you. Therefore, it is one of the ways that things must get done; slowly, methodically, and carefully. If Achiever® is in your top 10, and is one of your three executing strengths in your top 10, doing things systematically and as fast as possible is probably one of the ways that you believe is the right way. If you have Belief® or Responsibility®, then the right way is to be in alignment with your integrity, core values, or your mission statement.

As a dominant Executor, things must be done. There must be something tangible, physical that you can show to prove to me that something was completed. You can't approach a dominant Executor and say, "I got so much done," without telling them what measurable activity you did, or else they won't appreciate it.

Why is productivity dominant? Dominant Executors wake up every morning with an invisible, but totally real scoreboard floating above their head, and this scoreboard starts the day with a big fat zero. Immediately, they feel the need to get points on that board by completing tasks on their list. They already know that if they come back to bed without enough points, they feel bad. There is an emotional reaction to not seeing enough points on that board. Their best way of doing this is making lists, whether they're physical, in your head, or if you're a stacker. I met a person once who just stacks things on their desk with the most important things on top, and the least important on the bottom. Their physical list is just a stack.

Productivity must be honored with everything you do. Check things off the list: get points on the board. Some will make a list of the small things like, "brush your hair, shower, clean face, put on makeup, get dressed, etc." just to be able to cross them off of the list. Even better, if you do something that wasn't on the list, you add it, just to be able to cross it off the list!

In the process of checking off their list, they'll often realize they're the only ones "doing anything," and it makes them question why they're the only one that cares about productivity. "Why am I the only one doing anything around here?" is a common question. Ultimately, they'll keep checking things off their list, scoring points. The higher the score, the higher the satisfaction. Point, point, point!

If you have Achiever® in your top 10 strengths (and three executing as well) you hate doing anything and not receiving appropriate credit for your efforts. High Achievers especially hate it when their work goes unnoticed or taken for granted. Productivity must be measured so that when you go to bed at night, you see all those points on the board and you can sleep well. Dominant Executors must see productivity in everything they do, or they will hesitate. But, if you're a dominant Executor and you see the best way to get something done is going to lead to some sort of unproductivity, you will hesitate. For example, if there's a party going on and you're in charge of planning it, you prefer to be the only one planning it because that way you don't have to have conversations with other people that end up being unproductive conversations, where the other person talks about how they can't get their dog to poop, or their chickens to lay eggs or something. High Executors hate being sucked into conversations that are stagnant. Working means getting a lot of stuff done.

There's also a subset of Executors who prefer to do things with other people, because they can see how to get more done when other people are doing tasks with them, as long as the small talk doesn't detract from the tasks at hand. Executors need to see productivity so badly that they're willing to just completely give up connections and feelings because it just gets in the way. This is oftentimes one of the reasons you'll see a dominant Executor or even a dominant Influencer with the Empathy® strength low. They understand that relying on, looking at, or taking notice of other people's feelings becomes unproductive.

My favorite thing about Executors is the list making, because it's where your productivity and value really shines. Let's say someone asks for your help. Would it be far more helpful to just make lists of their problems for them? You can listen to them talk about their issues, and make lists of it all with all the ways you can help them get those things done, because that's what you're all about: productivity.

I love dominant Executors because we need them in our lives. I know I do. Honestly, there's no way I would have gotten so many things done in my life had I not been married to a dominant Executor. I'm grateful for her, because she showed me how to be productive. If it weren't for her, I would just be talking to people all day long and never get anywhere.

One of the Executing strengths is Belief®, which I've already alluded to. It's extremely powerful. If you have Belief® in your top 10 and you have three executing strengths, you need to do things in a way that honors your core values. All decisions about the "right way" are based on these core values. All of them. You can't just come up to a person with high belief and expect them to buy into your new ideas or your new ways of doing things. You see, with high belief, you come at this with so much skepticism. You want to make sure that what I'm teaching lines up with your core values before you begin to assimilate it. My hope is that you're reading this book because someone else told you it benefited him or her and you believe them. I know that you won't take any of this seriously until it lines up with your core values.

However, one problem with high belief is you haven't fully articulated or even identified what the core values actually are. Without identifying them, decision making can get fuzzy, which means you may naturally resist anything that is not in complete alignment with your core values; hence, you are sometimes labeled as "stubborn."

Whether you're a dominant Executor or not, whether or not you have three or more executing strengths in your top 10, I want you to think of all the stubborn people in your life and realize that maybe they're stubborn because they really do have a powerful set of values. All they want you to do is help them understand how what you're trying to teach them lines up with those core values. People of high belief must articulate what their values are, or it makes it harder for them to make decisions. So, if you have high belief and you've been resistant to this whole thing, I get it. It's totally cool. Be as resistant as you want. My challenge to you is to get clear about what your core values are when it comes to how people should be doing things, how people should be connected with, how people should be motivated, or how people should be creative. When you do, this will all make so much more sense to you.

The bottom line is if you have three or more executing strengths in your 10, stick to being productive. I'm thankful for the Executors, because they keep us all productive.

QUESTIONS:

HOW MANY EXECUTING STRENGTHS DO YOU HAVE IN YOUR TOP 10?

IF YOU HAVE HIGH BELIEF, HOW DOES THIS INFORMATION RESONATE WITH YOUR CORE VALUES?

WHO DO YOU KNOW WHO IS A DOMINANT EXECUTOR? HOW DOES THIS HELP YOU UNDERSTAND THEM BETTER?

CHAPTER 7
STRATEGIC THINKING STRENGTHS
"THINK, CREATE AND/OR LEARN"

Strategic Thinking is also a favorite of mine, because I have three of these in my top 10. Now, if you have three or more of the strategic thinking strengths in your top 10, the desire that must be honored with everything you do is to think, create, and/or learn. Let me say that again. The desire is to think, create, and/or learn. Now, the reason why I say that is because not all Strategic Thinkers like to learn, and not all Strategic Thinkers like to create, but all Strategic Thinkers like to think.

What is thinking? It's visualizing, it's analyzing, it's theorizing, it's strategizing, it's taking complex concepts and making them simple for other people to understand. Strategic Thinkers love to be in their head. They're energized by it. For example, if you have Intellection® as one of your top strengths, then you must know that there is a thought process behind everything. You love to go deep and really think about the meaning behind everything. People who have Intellection® high are very wise. They also need to know the why, the reason, behind things they are asked to do.

The bottom line with Strategic Thinkers is that they need space to use their minds. This is why a lot of people with three or more strategic thinking strengths need time alone; not always, and not a lot. It's just some time for them, and their thoughts. Consider scheduling alone time, or just uninterrupted time for you to be thinking or learning.

I want you to think about this for yourself. If you have three or more strategic thinking strengths in your top 10, think about how energized you are by the intellectual activity that you currently enjoy, or how the intellectual activity has diminished from what you currently do. Are you de-energized by what you do, because you don't have the space to think?

I used to work for a large corporation and it was really hard to get alone time to just think, because everything about that job was focused on productivity. I was a Strategic Thinker put into a room with a whole bunch of Executors who didn't understand that my thinking was highly productive.

Strategic Thinkers are highly productive when they're thinking. What often happens is that they think about what to do with such intensity that when it comes time to take action, be it connecting with others, getting things done or influencing others, they are highly efficient because they've thought about it so thoroughly.

Strategic Thinkers love to gather information for themselves and for other people especially when there's a purpose that excites them. For example, a dominant Strategic Thinker with three executing strengths will gather information that feeds efficiency and productivity. If you're a dominant Executor and a secondary Strategic Thinker, you love to gather information, to create more efficient methods, to make things faster. If you have three or more Relationship strengths alongside three Strategic Thinking, then you're gathering information about things that will help you connect more effectively with others. You gather information to learn more about people's emotions, to understand them on a deeper level. If you have three Influencing strengths and three Strategic Thinking, then the information you're gathering is about helping people move forward. You love to gather information to help other people move past their fears and blocks.

Dominant Strategic Thinkers who have a secondary relationship building will read books like *The Emotion Code*, or *Biology of Belief*. These are wonderful books for those who want to understand people at a deeper level. People who are dominant Strategic Thinkers and Executors will read books on efficiency: *The 12 Week Year* or *The Power of Habit*. Strategic Thinkers with secondary influencing will read books like *The Five Second Rule* or *The Big Leap*. These Strategic Thinkers have an external application for all the internal work. When they're not doing anything, Strategic Thinkers can get so much done by just going for a walk. Their mind is stimulated by information and they don't always show it.

As a dominant Influencer and Strategic Thinker, I spent a year and a half coaching thousands of people for free. My wife, the dominant Executor, never understood it. Before now, it seemed unproductive to her. Now she sees the value, and sees how my ability to gather information to help other people move forward has become a lucrative business. It's also helped our marriage. It's helped my ability to help my children. It's made me a better husband, and parent, and a far better provider for my family. My wife got a better husband when she let me have space to use my strategic thinking strengths even though she considered them unproductive.

So, remember, if you have three or more strategic thinking strengths, it's all about the thinking and the creating, or the learning to help facilitate the external application of one or two of the other three domains. I hope this helps you tremendously. Let's wrap up all these domains and make a statement to help you apply these desires to everything you do going forward.

QUESTIONS:

HOW MANY STRATEGIC THINKING STRENGTHS ARE IN YOUR TOP TEN?

WHAT RESONATES WITH YOU ABOUT THIS CHAPTER?

WHO DO YOU KNOW WHO IS A DOMINANT STRATEGIC THINKER? HOW DOES THIS HELP YOU UNDERSTAND THEM BETTER?

CHAPTER 8
THE STRENGTHS PROCLAMATION

We've now gone through all four of the domains: Relationship Building, Executing, Influencing, and Strategic Thinking. You're recognizing by now that you have certain desires that must be honored with everything you do. My hope is that you've read through all four of these chapters and realized which ones fit you, and that it's important to honor these desires for the rest of your life.

Let's make your Strengths Proclamation. You get to take these desires and make a proclamation to the world and to yourself. You get to own what it is you want most in a specific, affirmative statement that actually means something and actually resonates with your soul.

First, you need to identify your dominant domains by counting how many of each domain you have in your top 10. Those domains which have three or more strengths in your top ten are your dominant domains. For some of you, this will be very easy, and for others, it may be confusing, or even a little bit upsetting. You might even want to fight me on this, but I'm just going to ask you to give me a chance to help you understand the whole aspect of it. The purpose of the Strengths Proclamation is for you to say that you're only going to do everything in a way that honors your authentic desires.

Let's sum it up once more. The Relationship Builder's desire to connect with the "right people." The Influencer's desire is to move people forward. Executors want to make sure things are done the "right way." Strategic Thinkers want to think, create, and/or learn. It looks like this:

I love to do everything in a way that honors my desire to
_____ and _____.

You're going to fill in the blanks with your dominant desires, based on your top 10 strengths report. I'm going to share mine to help you create yours, and we'll talk about how it works. I have five influencing, three strategic thinking strengths, and two executing in my top 10. I won't use the executing strengths in my statement. I love to do everything in a way that honors my desire to move people forward, and think, create, and learn. That is my Strengths Proclamation. It is my statement to the world, and to me. It also gives me an answer to the question, "Who am I?"

If I was sitting in a room, being interviewed, and was asked to talk about myself, the first thing out of my mouth would be, "Well, my name is Eddie Villa, and I love to do everything in a way that honors my desire to move people forward and think, create, and learn." Isn't that powerful? See how I never brought up my marriage status, my seven kids, anything about my religion, race, job, or where I grew up? Instead, I get to talk about who I am as a person. That's who I am, and that's what makes me smile. My statement makes me happy. That's also how I do everything.

You are probably looking at your Strengths Proclamation at this point, and you're feeling one of two things: 1) "Yes! That is totally me!" or 2) "This doesn't make sense." So, let me help you understand why my proclamation works with everything, and yes, I do mean **everything**. I am putting high emphasis on "everything" for a reason, because I love to influence others in a way that honors my desire to move people forward and think, create, and learn. I love to be creative in a way that honors my desire to move people forward and think, create, and learn. I love to be productive in a way that honors my desire to move people forward and think, create, and learn. I also love to connect with people in a way that honors my desire to move people forward, and think, create, and learn.

You are reading this book because you want to find out how to be who you are with everything you do. It's time to own that. You love to do everything this way. I am only limiting you to the desires you have three or more of in your top 10. So, if you have seven relationship building strengths, two in another domain, and one in a third domain, then everything you do must be about connecting with the right people. I really want you to own that because it's so true. You love to do everything in a way that honors that one, single desire.

A lot of times, people will say things to me like, "Eddie. I have eight relationship building in my top 10, so how do I influence people with that? How am I supposed to get things done? How am I supposed to be creative?" I remind them that they forgot the golden rule: **Your strengths report has nothing to do with what you can or cannot do. It is how you do everything your way, and it works, but only 100% of the time.** Your influence is best done when you first connect with others. Your productivity is best done when you first connect with others. Your creativity is best done when you first connect with others. If you have eight relationship building strengths in your top 10, you do everything best when you start with connecting with people. What matters is that the desire must be honored with everything you do. So, when you make your Strengths Proclamation, you're only going to use the top 10 strengths that you have three or more of in any particular domain.

If you are having trouble with this, I suggest you look at how your Strengths Proclamation shows how you have ever been successful at anything in your life. A lot of times I run into people who think they're not Influencers, so I ask them questions. "Have you ever been married? Have you ever been employed? If so, then you're an Influencer." In fact, if you've ever convinced someone to marry you, even if it didn't end well, you are still a "closer." You convinced someone to give you a chance. If you've ever been hired after a job interview then you are a "closer," my friends. No matter what you do, everything must be done in a way that honors these desires so that you can be who you are at a high level with everything you do, thus getting results that energize you.

Do not ever forget the golden rule. Write it down to help you remember it: _____

_____

_____

_____ .

Now let's return to those of you with high belief. I know that you have a level of stubbornness, which is a good thing, by the way. It's important. If you have Belief® high, stop and ask yourself if your Strengths Proclamation lines up with your core values on how people should be treated, how things should be done, how creativity must take place, and/or how connections must happen.

If it does, then own it. The purpose of the Strengths Proclamation is for you to finally own who you are with everything you do, so that you can be who you are at every level.

There's a really cool thing called neuron mirroring. Neuron mirroring is something that came through an experiment. Two musicians, a violinist and a cellist were placed in a room and asked to collaborate on a piece. As they played, their neurons started firing in sync, because they were listening to each other, and anticipating each other's next notes. They were working in perfect partnership to create one sound. When they split the musicians up into different rooms, it changed their neurons. They were no longer playing in sync, because they were each trying to create their own sound with the piece of music. It was no longer one sound from two people. They were disconnected.

When you are you, with everything you do, then your neurons are firing in harmony with your highest desires. Ultimately, if you doubt who you are, or think it won't work, your brainwaves actually change. The people that you're with can sense the change.. They feel it, even if they can't articulate it, but they will become uncomfortable. They will question their trust in you, which means they won't want to be around you, they won't believe you, and it will create a level of doubt. You become less influential. When you stop being you, you become less productive, less creative, you disconnect from people that you want to connect with. When this happens, grab your Strengths Proclamation, and get back into the right headspace. When you do everything in your strengths, you make it easy to love who you are, easy to show people your value, and make it really easy for others to love and embrace who you are.

I hope that you read this with intent to love yourself and embrace your Strengths Proclamation with everything you do. If you're struggling with this, my suggestion is to review how your Strengths Proclamation has given you success in the past (even when you were not aware of it!). Review how you've had success by connecting with the right people, moving people forward, making sure things are done the right way, and thinking, creating, and/or learning. You'll then be able to find evidence on how to move forward with the same intentions

QUESTIONS:

WHAT IS YOUR STRENGTHS PROCLAMATION?

WRITE IT TWO OR THREE MORE TIMES FOR DIFFERENT AREAS OF YOUR LIFE (i.e. I LIKE TO IMPROVE MY MARRIAGE IN A WAY ....)

CHAPTER 9
THE CHAMELEONS

Let me address one hesitation that you could be having right now about your Strengths Proclamation. I'm speaking to you "Chameleons," you slippery, shapeshifters who are energized by trying to be everything for anyone.

You're the one in the crowd that is thinking, "But Eddie.... I like to connect with the right people AND I like to think, create, and/or learn AND I like to move people forward, AND I like to make sure things are done the right way.

So let me address this concept so you no longer hesitate. That's what's important, my friends, is that your strengths help you to stop hesitating.

There are some of you who, when you count the number of strengths domains in your top 10, it looks like one of these combos, where the numbers refer to how many of each domain you have in your top 10.

3 - 3 - 3 - 1
Ex. 3 Relationship Building, 3 Influencing, 3 Strategic Thinking, 1 Executing

3 - 3 - 2 - 2
Ex. 3 Influencing, 3 Strategic Thinking, 2 Relationship Building, 2 Executing

4 - 2 - 2 - 2
Ex. 4 Executing, 2 Influencing, 2 Relationship Building, 2 Strategic Thinking

4 - 3 - 3
Ex. 4 Strategic Thinking, 3 Executing, 3 Relationship Building

You might not feel like the Strengths Proclamation fully captures the complexity of your authentic desires because you really do appreciate elements of all four domains. What makes you such a powerful person is how you can "chameleon" into different roles.

You're the ultimate "utility player" like we say in baseball, or a "triple threat" as they say in the performing arts.

Here's what generally happens. You may be around a group of friends who you adore and you can easily play the relationship builder role. You can be involved in a group of people who are trying to complete a task and you can get focused on the task at hand. You might enjoy some alone time and really dive deep into learning, being creative or thinking about something profound. Or when push comes to shove, you're ready to help people take action, and move forward.

The important question is, "Which one do I start with?" By the way, the same question could be asked if you have four of one domain and four of another or five of one and five of another in your top 10.

Which one comes first? Remember in the chapters on Influencers and Relationship Builders we discussed how a Relationship Builder would not want to sacrifice connection to move someone forward and an Influencer would not want to sacrifice moving someone forward in favor of simply connecting. Stop and think "In which domain is my energy highest?"

Some environments might bring out certain elements of your strengths report more readily than others, but if you remember that there's still one domain, one desire that matters more than the others, at least you can step into that environment and "chameleon" into your true self.

Let me give you an example from someone close to me. He has three relationship building strengths in his top five and a mix of strategic thinking, influencing and executing in his top ten and has a combo of 3 RB -3 ST - 2 IN -2 EX. He's the ultimate utility player and can take on many different roles. But at the end of the day, where do I see him happiest? It's when he's hanging out and connecting with his "right people." Though he values productivity, he will sacrifice it for connection. Though he loves to think, create and/or learn, if he's not connecting with people he feels like he's too solitary. He loves to be with people. He will sacrifice moving someone forward if it risks the relationship.

He struggled to decide if Relationship Builder was his dominant domain. One thing that helped him decide that connecting with other people was his most important desire was by looking at his #6 strength WOO® (or Winning Others Over). He decided to consider his WOO® strength as a wild card, a joker, if you will, when counting up the strengths in each domain. People with high WOO® love to be around people in social situations. They particularly enjoy moving about the room and meeting new people. They tend to be gregarious and friendly. With that "wild card" strength he decided that he truly was a Relationship Builder.

I share that story with you to help you see both the simplicity of your strengths report and how we can over complicate it. I know my friend, I know he would much rather connect with people, but HE needed to decide where his energy was highest. He looked at his report and came to that unique conclusion based on his track record of success with people. It was his "aha moment" that came after some complicated mental gymnastics.

This is why I believe strengths coaching is so powerful, because it helps people see their infinite uniqueness and value based on THEIR report. Instead of a coach telling someone how to be or what to do, the coach can take these dominant desires and these strengths to help their client craft a plan that is 100% authentic to them, and has already given them success in the past.

In Chapter 11 we're going to be talking about your Strengths DNA, which is essentially the flow you create for yourself using your strengths. For those of you who have a bit of a chameleon profile, your Strengths DNA will be an important tool for you to find your flow.

The important thing is to remember that the purpose of Unleash Your Strengths is to stop hesitating, to stop feeling like who you are is not enough (or too much), and to settle into an understanding and love for who you are and what energizes you. These strengths have been behind every success, important connection, and every achievement and it's time to give them, and you, the credit they deserve.

QUESTIONS

ARE YOU A CHAMELEON? IF SO, HOW DOES THIS CHAPTER
RESONATE WITH YOU?

CHAPTER 10
THE ANCHOR STRENGTH

This chapter did not appear in the first edition of Unleash Your Strengths. It's a concept I reserved for my coaching clients and for members of the Unleash Your Strengths Community. But I'm going to give you a special preview into a concept that I learned after studying over one thousand strengths reports.

When I was going through my own journey of understanding strengths through discussing them with the people who had their reports, there was something I was noticing consistently. It became clear to me that there was always something holding people back when it came to their strengths. No matter how obvious the value of their strengths were to people there was always some intense form of fear that would come with it.

Let me preface by saying that when you look at the strengths from 1 to 34 you can know one thing. They are placed in order based on the amount of energy or resistance you feel towards using those strengths. Strengths one through ten represent high energy and low resistance. The bottom strengths (which we will cover in Chapter 12) are the strengths of high resistance.

A strengths report can be taken at face value the majority of the time. You took the report and you answered the questions. You told the assessment which strengths energized you and which ones you didn't enjoy using. The ones that are at the bottom from 27 - 34, you answered pretty immediately that you didn't like using that strength. You felt high resistance and you felt it pretty definitively. On the other hand, your top strengths were listed in that order based on your high energy for those strengths.

I discovered something insightful about the top ten strengths and that was a pattern that there was ONE strength, right smack dab in the middle, that always seemed to be the leader, the captain if you will, the one strength that could lead the charge.

That strength is your #5 strength.

Here's a really basic drawing to illustrate this principle.

#1 Strength
- Sargeant

#5 Strength
- Anchor
- Captain

#10 Strength

Your #5 strength is like the heart of your strengths report and every other strength follows the lead of your heart. They follow the intentions and desires of your #5 strength.

All of your strengths are like people; little soldiers that all have their own agenda. Your #5 is the captain, the one that they are all trying to appease. If your #5 strength isn't being honored, then all the other strengths go in multiple directions and get under utilized. That loss of direction leads you to hesitate to fully unleash them.

This means we get to be really clear about how our #5 strength honors our dominant domains and how the #5 helps us start our process of authenticity in everything we do.

Start by getting clear about your dominant domain. Write it out.

"I love to do everything in a way that honors my desire to _____
_____
_____.

Next, look at how your #5 strength is the captain, how it goes first. It's the one that tells you what to do first.

I've tested the theory on thousands of people and the response is nearly unanimous. They can see how that #5 Strength is the one that moves the others forward, that drives the train, or gives direction.

My #5 Strength is Self-Assurance® , which is a desire to follow an inner compass for oneself. For me that means I start with my "gut feeling".

My wife's #5 is Arranger®, so she leads with a desire to make sure all the things in her life are in the right place. She loves to have something to work with and put it together.

No matter what your #5 strength is, review the descriptions of that strength in your assessment and ask yourself how you've seen that strength be the one that really drives your train.

So what about your #1 strength? Well, #1 is the sergeant, the one that gets orders from the captain and tells the rest of the strengths how to do things.

As an example, let's say you're a dominant Relationship Builder and your #5 is Strategic® and your #1 is Positivity®, then you love to do everything in a way that honors your desire to connect with the right people. You do this best by looking for all the best possible options of people to connect with and choose the best ones. Then you move forward with those people with enthusiasm, joy, and a light hearted, cheerful attitude. Then all the rest of your strengths come next.

What I love about this framework is that it boils your top strengths down to three important concepts:

1. Your dominant domain
2. Your #5
3. Your #1

Doing so helps us more efficiently remove the "leashes" that can hold us all back.

Imagine if you started off your day convinced that in order to be yourself at the highest level, all you have to do is those three things. How would it change your life to begin right there?

Understanding strengths is both easy and extremely deep. There are so many amazing nuances about how each strength interacts with each other and within the confines of your dominant domain. However, you can simplify your top strengths just by going straight to those three items on your report.

It is my mission to help you move through life more energized. My concern is that in my pursuit of a deep understanding of strengths, I make this too complicated and it doesn't get you moving. I lay awake at night trying desperately to make this simple for you because this conversation about strengths is pointless if you aren't creating results that excite you.

Use these simple steps to help you understand everything about what makes you unique and wonderful. There is nothing more to life than giving that to others.

QUESTIONS:

WHAT DO YOU LOVE ABOUT YOUR YOUR #5? WHAT DOES THE #5 MEAN TO YOU BASED ON GALLUP'S® DESCRIPTION?

HOW DOES YOUR #5 HELP YOU HONOR YOUR DOMINANT DOMAIN?

HOW CAN YOU USE YOUR #5 STRENGTH TO GET THE TRAIN ROLLING?

CHAPTER 11
YOUR STRENGTHS DNA

Are you ready to learn something so powerful that it's going to change the way you see yourself? It's going to change the way everyone else sees you. It's the biggest secret that I'm going to share in this book. If you only read one chapter, make this it, because it is going to improve so much for you, not only in your self confidence, but also in your health, relationships, and income.

Consider how we've been taught to believe in ourselves. One of the things I have to laugh at (sorry) is how I used to try and believe in myself many years ago. I hated who I was for a long time, and when I wanted to change that about myself, I listened to a bunch of gurus explain mantras. They'd say, "Look in the mirror and compliment yourself, saying good things like, you are wonderful. Everybody loves when you speak. You are perfect just the way you are." I realized that these were not actually uplifting for me.

The fact is that it's so easy to compare ourselves to other people. We've talked about this before. The only person worth comparing yourself to is who you once were. Everyone else is infinitely unique and has a different set of strengths than you do. Comparison is irrelevant. Frequently we look in the mirror and try to affirm ourselves by saying things that we would like to be, "You're charismatic! You're an inspirational public speaker! You're the leader of a multi-million dollar organization!"

You may become all of those things in time, but there's no step by step process in the affirmation, nothing that tells you how. Well, your strengths report tells you how, and your Strengths DNA is your step by step, affirmation. Perfect right? Best of both worlds!

The Strengths DNA is so much fun! I have one more thing to share before I show you how to create it. A lot of us are conditioned to believe that we need to develop our weaknesses. When we look at the things that we are not, our natural instinct is to try to make our weaknesses better. My goal is to turn you against that. It's going to be frustrating, but as we go into this section of Strengths DNA, it will become clear. Then as we go into the next chapter on your bottom strengths, you'll see even more clearly why it's not worth it.

Pay attention to how simple this process is. When it comes to DNA, it stands for your strength's Dominant Natural Actions. It's your DNA, which means it's encoded into who you are. It's how you flow perfectly with everything that you do in success. One of the biggest travesties about success is that when we do things well, it's so much easier for us to believe it was a fluke, or freak occurrence, and not just because we are stellar at what we do, and how we do it. When you're reading this book, or when you're hanging out with me, listening to me talk about strengths, understand that I will always give you credit for the success you've done in your life by looking at your strengths.

So when you try to create affirmations or mantras that are not based on your strengths, they can feel like lies. Fake it until you make it, really means, "Be fake until you make it." There is no action in this statement. It's weird. It bothered me because it never gave me something to look for when it came to my value. I can sit and stare in a mirror all day telling myself that I could have rock hard abs. Plenty of people have abs, so why not you? It doesn't really matter if that's true or not. If I don't believe it in my heart of hearts, it's not going to happen. It leads me to look at my chubby belly that looks more like Jello® and think, "yeah right!" Well, that is going to lead me to eating a donut to make myself feel better.

My point is that lies don't lead to action. What really leads to action is finding proof. Finding proof. You see, your maker has created something inside of you that is amazing. It's called the reticular activating system. Think about all of the information that constantly bombards you. Lights, colors, sounds, smells, touches, tastes, everything; it's a constant barrage of data. There are billions and billions of data points constantly trying to come into your eyes, ears, nose, mouth, and onto your skin. If your brain actually paid attention to every single bit of information that was coming at you, your head would explode.

It's too much. Your reticular activating system filters out things, and only allows in what is important. That's it, only what is important. You have to be asking yourself at this point what is deemed important information. That's the secret. You choose it every morning. You decide. You choose it. Every day you get to pick and choose what is important information and what is not. Think about when you're driving down the same streets you've seen numerous times. You don't look at the signs, because you know what they are already. So, it's deemed unimportant. Everything you see is what you've decided matters. The reticular activating system also decides what you will believe about yourself.

That's got to be hitting hard right now. Think about this: every opinion you have of yourself is based on evidence that you are choosing to allow through the filter of your reticular activating system. Everything you've done in your life, whether good or bad, you have chosen to consider important, or trash. If it's natural for us to think that success is accidental, then we never look at success as being a part of us, because we are too busy looking at our weaknesses and failures. When we focus on our failures, we bring in stress, fear, and a resistance to vulnerability. My friends, you have the recipe for getting out of being stuck, and it is all a choice.

The reticular activating system is there to help you decide what's important. The great news is that every time you look for something bad, you have the same capacity to look for something good. If you are naturally conditioned to look at the bad, it will take a conscious effort to focus on the good. So, right here in this chapter, I've got a challenge for you. I want you to think of a fews wins that you've had in the last three months, big or small.

1. _____

2. _____

3. _____

You'd be surprised at how hard this is for some people. If you're not able to think of something automatically, then be aware that it's time to condition your mind to look for the good in yourself. You are missing your wins.

It's okay if you're getting emotional right now. How many wins have you had over the last three months? _____ Come on, you cannot sit here and tell me that you have done nothing good. We both know it's a big fat lie. Give yourself some credit. What are three small wins you've had? What we're going to do is use your amazing reticular activating system to start filtering out those failures and start filtering in your successes.

I hope you've thought of your successes. It doesn't matter if it's big or small. Stop looking for situations where you change the world, okay? How about a time that you helped a friend, helped yourself, or maybe even did something really good when it comes to health, relationship, income, or self-belief? Success can come on so many levels. I want you to think about that great thing you did because I'm going to share with you what I do every single day.

Let's talk about how the Strengths DNA comes into play. When I look at myself in the mirror, or when I'm standing in the shower, I tell myself a mantra that is based on reality that my reticular activating system gets to use as a way of filtering all of the good in my reality. The truth about my value is found, because I filter my reticular activating system to find my value. The best way I do it is with my Strengths DNA, my Dominant Natural Actions.

I'm going to share mine with you, and I want you to think about yours. It is my Strengths Proclamation (I love to do everything…) and then I go right into my DNA. For me, I use my top 13 strengths, because that's where I am best. Here's how I do it. Imagine being back in that interview room and being asked to tell the interviewer about yourself. Here is how I answer that question: "My name is Eddie (and I recite my Strengths Proclamation). I love to do everything in a way that honors my desire to move people forward and to think, create, and learn."

Then here comes my Strengths DNA. I start with my #5 and say,

"How I do this best is I trust myself and believe in my inner compass that points me in the right direction (#5 - Self Assurance®) even if I make mistakes. I see multiple ways of doing things and I pick the best one. (#1 - Strategic®). I get excited about taking action, and I connect with others to move them forward (#2 - Activator®) in a way that honors my vision of the future (#3 - Futuristic®) that excites me and puts me into action. I make new friends along the way and entertain others (#4 - WOO®), while I gather information to improve who I am to make me better (#6 - Learner®). I speak from the heart with great enthusiasm to move people forward (#7 - Communication®) and I do it better than anyone else because I do it my way (#8 - Competition®). I lay out the steps towards the direction that I want to go (#9 - Focus®) and I put all of the pieces and people together for maximum productivity (#10 - Arranger®). I then gather more information for other people (#11 - Input®) while I make sure that we are on a path towards what we want in our lives (#12 - Achiever®). I do all of this in a way that's going to change the world" (#13 - Significance®.

You see what I did there? I made a Strengths Proclamation. I said something about my #5 Strength. Then I said something about my #1 Strength and then I said something about every other strength from 2 - 13 in a cohesive affirmation that actually honors who I am!

Imagine the look on someone's face when asking the simple question "Tell me about yourself," and imagine confidently reciting your own Strengths DNA? You see, what's awesome is I never had to bring up my family, my religion, my race, or anything else. That creed is who I am. My Strengths DNA is how I do everything, and it works, but only 100% of the time. So, when I look in the mirror and I've got this thing that I want to overcome, maybe the fear of standing in front of thousands of people, or releasing a book to the world that I know will make a difference, I stop. I recite my proclamation and DNA, and all of my strengths come into play. There is no confusion when it comes to my top strengths. I lay out my #5, then I lay out the rest in sequential order, because I know that my DNA is best when I do it this way. It's an affirmation based on truth.

When I speak truth to myself, I can see how many times in my life that it has worked. I'm only sad that I never saw it before. I'll never make that mistake again. When you lay out your DNA, it's concise and obvious. It's time to review your top 10 strengths and write out your DNA. Find the short descriptions of each top 10 strength, and reformulate them into short expressions or little bites of information that flow from one to the next. Always keep in mind your domain and how each strength helps you honor your domain. Remember the dominant domains and their desires:

Relationship Building: connecting with the right people
Influencing: move people forward
Executing: getting things done the right way
Strategic Thinking: thinking, creating, and/or learning

I want you to start with just the #5 and the #1 and see how that flows with your Strengths Proclamation. Then add numbers 2-4 and 6-10. Mine went to Strength #13, and you can end your DNA at a spot where you feel the energy diminish. That could be at 11, 12, 13, 14 or even 15. But make sure you do at least your top 10.

Take your time with it. Mine has become part of who I am, and every time I speak it, it is slightly different. It shifts a little bit, but I can always apply it. If I'm heading to hang out with my kids: "I love to hang out with my kids in a way…" If I'm heading on a date with my wife: "I love to go on dates with my wife in a way…" If I'm going on stage to speak: "I love to speak on stage in a way…" Always. The Strengths DNA shows me exactly how I'm going to do it, and I get fired up every time. You can probably feel my energy right now.

Here's your opportunity to start your DNA for yourself. Try and get your first five strengths written down before going to the next chapter, because we're going to turn everything on it's head and take you down the path of what it's like to live in your bottom strengths. It's not fun.

Here is my challenge to you before you go through this exercise. Take a look at one area of your life where you are already doing well; your health, your relationships or your income. Use this DNA statement to help you see why you are already doing well. This isn't a one time exercise. You won't get this right the first time. Keep at it. Keep practicing. Keep reciting. Get it ingrained into your reticular activating system so you begin to default into your dominant natural actions based on who you actually are.

We have all been conditioned to only see where we are falling short in life and that has not contributed to us being who we are at a higher level. THIS IS THE MOST VALUABLE COMPONENT TO

STRENGTHS. Find proof you are enough!

Here's your template to fill out your Strengths DNA:

I love to
(the thing you want to do)_____
in a way that honors my desire to
(dominant desire)_____
and
(secondary desire) _____.

I do this best when I am:

5. _____

And then I:

1 _____

2 _____

3 _____

4 _____

6 _____

7 _____

8 _____

9 _____

10 _____

CHAPTER 12
BOTTOM STRENGTHS

Before I get into these bottom strengths, I really need to give you a disclaimer. I want you to understand that this discussion of the bottom strengths can be very confusing, thus frustrating. When we discuss the bottom strengths, it is a discussion about what physically drains you, what emotionally disconnects you from other people, and what keeps you from being productive and creative. So, I want you to know that as we discuss this, and as I start breaking down the rules of the bottom strengths, any frustration, confusion, or anger you feel is normal. So, be ready. It's not always going to be pretty, and it won't always be clear, but just understand that these strengths are what you want to stay away from.

The best way to understand the bottom strengths is to backtrack to hesitation. When we're trying to do something, no matter what it is; improve our health, relationships, income, or our belief in ourselves, the simple actions that are required stop when we hesitate. We hesitate because we truly believe that being who we are is not going to work. The only thing that we know how to do when we're not being who we are is to be the opposite. I want you to think about this for yourself. How many times have you ever made the decision that just being who you are isn't going to work? So, instead, you just, sort of, be someone that you're not. You end up being your weaknesses, which is exactly who you are NOT. It doesn't make any sense. Just be your weaknesses? Nobody does that!

The best analogy I've ever given on this is the hammers and ham sandwiches story. Imagine that you're in a room with a table full of hammers that represent your top 10 strengths. On another table are five ham sandwiches, which are your bottom strengths. Your goal is to drive a nail through a 2x4 board. Which one of these tools are you going to pick up? The hammer, of course. Now, I know this sounds stupid, because it is very obvious. But, I'm looking at you right now, and I'm thinking about you, and I'm thinking about all of the people I've helped. The truth is, we all try to pick up the ham sandwiches. We try to be something we're not in order to get something that we want, because we have all been convinced that who we are is not enough. So, we start off using the hammer. We're working hard to pound that nail in, and we're getting tired. Because we're tired, we've figured that we should try something else, because it's not working.

So now, you're standing in front of this block of wood with a nail in it holding a ham sandwich. It's filled with pickles, lettuce, mayo, and ham, turkey, maybe some salami, and tomatoes, nice tasty bread, and it's huge. It's messy. You try making this ham sandwich pound the nail. Instead, it creates a bigger mess, so you grab a couple of the sandwiches, balling them up to make one big mass, to use as force against the nail. You're getting exhausted trying to drive this nail into the wood. There's lettuce and ham flying everywhere, and the nail keeps going through and hitting the palm of your hand. You've developed a welt and it's bleeding. Picture this. This is exactly what we do. We try harder and harder, thinking that if we try and be someone we're not, we'll succeed.

Okay, so, it's epically failing, and in walks a friend of yours, seeing your hand bleeding, and your ham sandwiches destroyed everywhere. What goes through their mind as they survey this huge mess? How do you think they're going to feel seeing you act that way, knowing that it is not who you truly are. What are they going to say to you? "Stop! What are you doing? What happened to your hand? Why are you using these sandwiches when the hammers are right there? What were you thinking?" But, you look at them and say, "No! I've got this. This is totally going to work. You don't know what you're talking about. It's just a flesh wound." You're sweating, fighting, and flailing.

This is exactly what it's like to live in your bottom strengths. It's a nightmare. What I want you to understand is that there are signs that you're doing it wrong. First you'll notice a physical drain on your body. Before the drain, your brain created a thought, a false thought that you didn't even notice. Because we don't connect that unconscious thought to the physical drain, we pawn off our fatigue on something else, like lack of sleep or someone else in your life who's making you do this. You start thinking that this goal you had is not for you even though you had the hammers all along to get it done and make it happen. You blame your stress, your eating habits, your spouse, your kids, your job, your neighbors, or God instead of getting to the root of the problem.

The harder we push, and the more we use the ham sandwiches, the deeper we're drained, and the worse it gets. The next thing that happens is we start doing things that are inauthentic to who we are. If you're a dominant Relationship Builder, you start doing things that disconnect you from other people. Influencers get in the way of people's growth, churn and burn through the people they're working with, or they give up and write them off. Executors become unproductive, or focus on doing other tasks that aren't connected to their bigger goals and dreams. Strategic Thinkers become uncreative, think unproductive thoughts, or they convince themselves they still don't know enough to be successful. In essence, you become the opposite of who you are meant to.

You end up displaying all of these opposite traits in front of someone you know, which makes them feel uncomfortable. You act weird. People are intuitive, and they feel weird vibes around you. It's not who you are. The bottom five strengths are a drain on you, but also on the people around you, because they don't know how to act when you are being inauthentic. I call it the "bottom five drain." Stay away from it!

I discovered this for myself when I started to realize there were a lot of things that I wanted to do in my life that really excited me. I wanted to create a large group of people that helped the world love themselves through their strengths. I didn't know what was happening, but in my mind, I started to tell myself how I was not going to be the person who would be good enough to do that. Even though I was the only one who saw what I saw when it came to strengths, I was willing to convince myself that I wasn't the right person for this job to create the thing that I knew needed to be created. As I went through the process of creating my group, there were a lot of physical drains that I worked through.

I would try to convince myself that I didn't want to rock the boat; I didn't want to offend people. I would think about ways to do things that wouldn't push people too hard, because I was worried that my love for strengths was too intense. I would do things to avoid conflict. Guess what? My number 34 is Harmony®. You guessed it! When I try to do things to avoid conflict, it is awful. It's exactly like the rest of us. My hands are full of mayo and ham, and they are bleeding, while the nail waits patiently to be pounded into the 2x4. If I try to use Harmony® in front of you, you will want to get away from me immediately. It's weird.

We become weird when we are trying to be something we're not. So, here's my challenge to you. Take a look at your bottom five strengths, from 30-34. Think about how when you use those strengths, they get in your way, and your highest desires, which you want to honor, become obsolete. For me, Harmony® gets in my way of moving people forward, creating, thinking, and learning. I cannot do any of those things if I'm worried about what other people will or won't think. Does that make sense to you? Just look at the descriptions that Gallup® has provided for you, and ask yourself what happens if you use these five bottom strengths and how do they get in your way.

Below are some spaces for you to write down your bottom 5 strengths, the short description of the strength, and then reflect on what happens when you use them.

30. _____
How does it get in your way?

31. _____
How does it get in your way?

32. _____
How does it get in your way?

33. _____
How does it get in your way?

34. _____
How does it get in your way?

How do they keep you from getting things done the way you love to do them? We're going to break down the things that happen that lead you to dip into your bottom strengths. Before that, I want to arm you with some knowledge that will help you shift out of this chapter and into the next one. Simply look at those bottom five and understand the power that they have to kick you down. Understand how they get in your way of your dominant domain. Do not be frustrated with feeling frustrated. It is normal to feel confused and lost right now: hence, the warning at the start of this chapter. We're going to go a little bit deeper, but I promise to pull you out shortly!

QUESTIONS:

WHAT HAPPENS WHEN YOU USE YOUR HAM SANDWICHES?

HOW DO YOU SEE YOURSELF DIPPING INTO YOUR BOTTOM
STRENGTHS WHEN YOU ARE HESITATING?

CHAPTER 13
TRIGGERS

Most people who talk about strengths don't emphasize the Bottom Strengths Dip like I do. Most people refer to the bottom strengths simply as the tools you never use. I found this to be quite the opposite of reality. People are always looking for a way to use their bottom strengths. How do I know this? Because when most people get their strengths report they glance at the first couple strengths, then glance at the bottom ones and immediately start thinking, "Well, I can't do _____ because these are my bottom strengths."

There's an obsession about the bottom strengths because we obsess over who we are not, what we cannot do, who we cannot become, and why we cannot do it. As a result there are many different ways that we can be triggered to dip into our bottom strengths. Keep in mind that these are general and affect everyone in different ways. I'm going to get specific about how they affect me to give you some frame of reference. But, essentially we are all affected by these triggers. As I break them down, I want you to think about each aspect of your life that matters: the stuff that means the most to you right now; your health, belief in self, income, and relationships. I want you to think about how the following four triggers send you into your bottom strengths: Fear, Stress, Vulnerability and Comparison.

FEAR

"False. Evidence. Appearing Real. F.E.A.R."

I'm sorry. Let me just roll my eyes a little bit. We have been conditioned to believe that fear is so bad. We're taught our brains are lying to us. Does that saying make you feel inspired to challenge your fears? Have you ever felt like that is the truth that puts you into action? Personally, I've never really embraced this description of fear, because it's never inspired me. It's only forced me to dislike myself, and the way my brain works. It's forced me to hate and reject the way I naturally react to things that I care about. It makes me feel isolated and ashamed that I feel afraid.

The secret that I learned is that fear shows up whenever I want to do something that is really important to me. If fear is always going to show up, how can it be a bad thing? It has to be valuable. Otherwise, I'm always going to reject my natural response to the things that I care about. Does that make sense to you? "False evidence appearing real," is a message to you and me that your brain is lying. We are conditioned, therefore, to believe our brain is lying to us. How inspiring is that?

Now, you may disagree with me on this point, but follow me. I have a little more that I want to talk about. I want you to think about the area of your life where you feel like you're struggling the most.

This is obviously the area of your life that you care about a lot, or else you wouldn't be struggling, correct? For example, if you have no interest in being a dentist, you don't struggle with learning about dental care. So, there's no fear. The only fear you have when it comes to dental care is whether or not your teeth are healthy enough to keep you from pain, but that's a different story. So, what I'm saying here is fear will only show up when you're in situations where you want something really badly. Fear shows up to stop you. The reason that fear is there is to keep us from doing things that are going to physically harm us.

For example, if you're walking down the street and you see traffic, fear of being hit will keep you from walking into oncoming traffic because that could cause injury, death or accidents. It's important to you to avoid injury, death and accidents. However, fear also reacts the same way to imagined dangers. For example, if you have a fear of public speaking, obviously getting on the stage is not something that is physically dangerous, but if you tell a story in your head about what is going to happen if you walk on stage you create an imagined danger. Your body will react the same way as if you were going to walk into traffic. This is how I learned that fear was a good thing. It let me know what I wanted to do meant something important to me, and it was coming up with ways to prove to me that I could get hurt. Think about every good thing you've ever done in your life. Think about all the times you've ever had success. Did you ever notice that you had fear, yet you proceeded forward?

Most often, it was because your desire to do the thing outweighed your fear. Fear always shows up when you care. So, If you're going to care, you have to welcome fear. It's part of the game. Fear is not false. It's your natural, emotional response to doing something that matters. So much good can come from you moving forward, despite those fears. The way people typically respond to fear is they shut it out, lock it in a closet, and pretend it isn't real.

What you don't realize is that fear is actually in that closet, working out, like a prison inmate who has nothing better to do but pump iron in the courtyard all day to pass time. It's full of tattoos and it looks mean, and it keeps getting stronger and stronger, the longer it's locked away, until it's so strong that it breaks down the door and holds you back from everything you really want to do. Every time you do something important, it will come in and kick you in the stomach and knock you down, and guess what? You're in control the whole time. You are actually the one that created it.

Let me offer you an alternative when it comes to dealing with fear. Assume that fear is always going to show up when you care the most. That means that when fear shows up, you're about to do something really important. We can't screw

this up. We have to do the thing that we care about in our strengths. We need to make sure they're shiny, polished, and ready to be used when the fear begins to rear its ugly head.

I want you to pretend that fear is showing up simply because you care. Fear always gets to be your partner because the thing you are doing matters to you. So imagine you're getting in the car, driving towards your destination, to this goal that you want. Don't put fear in the backseat, and definitely do not let fear drive. Put fear right where it belongs, in the passenger seat, right by your side.

I am writing this book to help you, for your benefit, but also because I want to help the world. You know what I'm afraid of though? I'm afraid that the people that you try to share this with are going to look at me and judge me, and not give this book a try, even though it will help them. I am terrified they're going to use their own judgments of me to get in their way of this information. I'm terrified, but I have two choices. I can try and pretend I'm something I'm not in order to get those people's attention, which will drain me, or I can just be who I am at a higher level and tell the whole world I'm scared, but I'm going to do it anyway. I want you to think about how that statement that I just made to you helps you understand me just a little better and maybe help you connect with me a little bit more. When we do our important work, and let people know we're doing it despite being afraid, we create action, we create community, and we create connection. We create influence, and we do it in a way that is authentic to who we are.

When we are triggered by fear, it can either put us into our bottom strengths, or it can put us in our top ones. In order for it to put us into the top strengths, we have to make the decision that fear is part of the game. It's a welcomed part. It's a partner; it's not in charge, it's just part of the game.

STRESS

A lot of people are constantly taught that stress is a bad thing. When I use the word, "stress" with you, can you feel that natural recoil? "Ooh, that's bad. Oh, we've got to keep away from stress. The more stressed I get, the worse things will get."

My grandfather, my dad, and my brother all died before the age of 55 due to heart disease. Stress is something that I am constantly concerned with, because I'm aware of how stress can affect the body. There's nothing wrong with that, except for one thing. It's how I perceive stress. So, if I get stressed out, then my natural reaction is to calm down, slow down, pull back, stop caring so much, and stop trying so hard to push ahead. Ultimately, what stress can do is trigger us into going into our bottom strengths because we're worried that being who we are will cause physical damage to us. Stress is like water filling a water balloon and you are the balloon. It keeps filling and filling until the balloon eventually reaches capacity and pops.

This is what we're all afraid of when it comes to stress. Now, the cool thing is that we are not balloons. We can expand. We don't have a limit on what can overstress us. Think about it. Look at how things you stressed about as a child no longer bother you. You have expanded. Let's look at stress as a good thing that allows us to expand. Instead of allowing stress to push us into our bottom strengths, we can stop and ask ourselves, "I'm feeling stressed. How can I expand my mind? How can I expand my emotional capacity? How can I expand my skills so this thing is no longer a stressor in the future?"

Stress is part of growth. When you go to a gym to push weight, you are putting stress on your muscles to the point that they physically break down and tear. As you keep working, the muscles regenerate and become stronger. You expand your capacity, which makes your muscles bigger. What happens if you quit? When you get stressed out, muscles shrink. That's where stress becomes a problem. It's not stress itself, but how we react to it that is the issue. When we give into stress and quit, we end up rolling back instead of looking for opportunities to expand. That's why I love stress. When I feel stress, I stop and ask myself how I can expand my mind, emotions, and skills. My goal is to make my current stressors irrelevant in the future by expanding.

That, my friends, is how we grow, and we use our top 10 strengths to do it. Why? Because if we are using our top 10 strengths even when we feel stressed, we actually become energized in the process. Imagine stress energizing you.

VULNERABILITY

The third trigger is vulnerability. This is probably one of the biggest ones, because many of us see vulnerability as being weak. To express to another person that I am flawed is an admission that I am broken or there's something wrong with me. I can tell you, without a doubt, that my father and my brother were both taught that vulnerability is weakness. I never once saw either of them cry or admit that they were wrong. It's something that always bothered me as a young man, because I felt like I had to be perfect. I'm not sure if this is a male thing, but I know for a fact that it's a human thing. When we are struggling or we are facing adversity in our lives, the last thing we want to do is tell the world. What I've learned is that vulnerability is massively powerful.

One of my favorite authors on this subject is Brene Brown and her book, Daring Greatly. "Tell the world, 'Here I am, strong, and flawed. Please accept me for who I am. I'm praying that you'll accept me without judgment.'" I love that so much, because it's like going up to people and saying, "Here's a weapon. You can use it on me, but I believe you never will." That's powerful because it gives the other person a chance to connect with me. Think about this. When I shared with you earlier about my fear, which is genuine, did you feel a deeper connection with me?

I'll give you another one of my fears. I'm definitely afraid of being the most amazing person when it comes to strengths. I am terrified of being the expert that is put on the pedestal of the world when it comes to strengths, because I have seen how people in our society treat people who are highly successful. They look for ways to tear them down, and that is a fear that I have. However, I have two choices. When I think about fear, I can either pull back, or keep going ahead. My friends, I could pull back right now, but I'm heartbroken over that idea, because that would mean that you don't get the value of what I've learned. So, I get to share with you that I'm scared of how you're going to treat me when I show up as an expert, not just in strengths, but also in network marketing, wealth, family, marriage, or any other area in my life I choose to show up in as an expert. I am terrified of how you're going to try and bring me down, because of how you think about yourself or how you judge you.

I'm sharing that fear with you. Do you consider me weak? Or do you recognize that I am someone like you? Flawed. Doing my best, but talented. Are you connecting with me more? My hope is that you'll instill this idea that vulnerability is nothing like weakness. It has power. It has strength. But, when we allow vulnerability to trigger us into being in our bottom strengths, we end up doing the opposite. We end up lying. We end up doing things that my father and brother did, which holds back what is great about us. And that, my friends, is the biggest travesty of this whole thing.

COMPARISON

I alluded to this earlier and now I want to drive home the point. You are infinitely unique. There is no one on earth that has your top 10 strengths in the same order as you. Couple that uniqueness with your unique life experiences, desires and perspectives, and there is no one on earth like you.

That should give you hope. That means when you feel the calling to do something outside of your comfort zone, or to do something that's either never been done by anyone else, or never done in the way you would like to do it, you've received a calling. You have a message based on these unique perspectives, life experiences, desires and strengths you have.

What happens though, is you look around at anyone who's ever tried to do that thing or a similar thing and you compare yourself to them. You think, "I can't do it because I don't have _____ or I am not _____." These comparisons trigger us. They shut us down. They send us into our bottom strengths. This leads to us becoming and acting inauthentic.

Instead of comparing yourself to others and getting triggered, compare yourself to who you once were. Think about how who you are today is more capable and confident than the person you were one year, three years or ten years ago. Consider how you're not afraid of the same things you used to be afraid of. Reflect on how your stressors have caused you to expand. The only person worth comparing yourself to is who you once were. That is where you will always find proof that you can be, do and have more. Now that you have your strengths you can see precisely how every time you were successful, you were using your strengths, and every time you struggled you were likely dipping into your bottom strengths.

These four triggers, fear, stress, vulnerability and comparison, send us into our bottom strengths. The good thing is that there is a way out of it, to shift back into the top. I'm hoping that you've experienced frustration and confusion in these last two chapters, because we are about to fly high into the next realm, and to sky-rocket you and propel you forward. It's like Superman. Once we make this shift, you are going to have a clearer understanding of what your bottom strengths really are, and why it's a place you want to stay away from, permanently.

QUESTIONS:

WHAT ARE YOU AFRAID OF? HOW DOES THAT DEMONSTRATE WHAT'S IMPORTANT TO YOU?

HOW HAS YOUR ABILITY TO HANDLE STRESS EXPANDED OVER THE YEARS? HOW CAN IT CONTINUE TO EXPAND IN YOUR STRENGTHS?

HOW HAVE YOU BEEN TRIGGERED TO DIP INTO YOUR BOTTOM STRENGTHS BY FEAR, STRESS, VULNERABILITY OR COMPARISON?

CHAPTER 14
BOTTOM STRENGTHS DNA

By now, you should have written your Strengths DNA, or at least the first few strengths in your DNA. You have before you a step by step list not only of who you want to be but how you want to be. Now we're going to do the exact same thing, just with your bottom strengths. This will really slam home that you are not your bottom strengths.

This is how I like to transition from my Strengths DNA top strengths to my bottom ones. It works like this. At my 13th strength, which is Significance® for me, I say, "I will do that in a way that will make an impact on the world." Then I transition into the Bottom Strengths DNA by saying:

"I can't do those things that way if I...," and then I go into my bottom five strengths, which I stay away from using. My #29 is Restorative™, which is focusing on what's broken to make it better. So here it goes:

"I can't do these things if I focus on what's broken to make it better, treat everybody the same (Consistency®), focus on my past (Context®), overthink (Deliberative®), or try to avoid conflict (Harmony®)." That's it, that's my Bottom Strengths DNA. It makes it so clear what I need to let go of, my friends.

I'm going to challenge you right now to make sure you have your Strengths DNA laid out, your Bottom Strengths DNA, and understand them just as well as you understand your top ones. Understanding those bottom five strengths will always give you the power to stay in your high strengths.

This chapter is meant to be short because you are not meant to spend a lot of time on your bottom strengths. I just want to formulate your Bottom Strengths DNA.

One more important tip. Don't focus on the word that Gallup® chose to label the strength. Too many people look at the word and completely misunderstand it. What's important about the bottom five strengths story is to help you understand that the words they chose are just words. It's the strength itself that we want to release. So, if you have something like Consistency® or Discipline® or Achiever® in your low strengths, understand those are just words that Gallup® chose. It doesn't mean that you can't achieve, be consistent, or disciplined. In fact, those strengths have almost nothing to do with those things. What we're doing is looking at the bottom five strengths description so that you can let go of them when you contrast them to your top strengths.

So, here's your challenge. Formulate your Bottom Strengths DNA. Transition with "I can't do those things if I..." and then you read the short descriptions of your bottom strengths, and that's it. That's all you have to do. Do this to give yourself the power to understand them, and to rid yourself of them, and release them. Let them go be with other people who find them valuable because they're not who you are.

QUESTION:

WHAT ARE YOUR BOTTOM STRENGTHS?

PUT TOGETHER YOUR BOTTOM STRENGTHS DNA. (HINT: I can't do this if I'm ....)

CHAPTER 15
YOUR STRENGTHS LIBERATION STATEMENT

One of the talents I've developed over the years from working with people one on one is to help someone understand the very essence of their strengths report within just a few minutes. I'm eternally grateful for this gift as it helps me move people forward, think, create and learn, connect with the right people, and make sure things are done the right way.

In 2021, I started my own coaching certification program, aptly named the "Eddie Villa Coaching Certification." One of these days I'll come up with a more creative one but for now the truth will do.

I don't certify people in strengths, that's Gallup's® job. However, I certify people in my unique way of coaching people, which not only includes strengths, but many other frameworks I have created, refined, and learned from seeing others create results for themselves.

In the process of teaching people how to break down a strengths report to its very essence I needed a framework to give my clients to help them see the patterns I intuitively saw. I'm going to give you this framework here in my book so you can begin to have an impact on people in your life. I want to help you set yourself free and set others free through this amazing framework called the Strengths Liberation Statement®.

A strengths report can be viewed through the lens of FOUR key components. In Chapter 10 I taught you the first three very clearly. Now I'm adding ONE more piece to make it abundantly clear how these four pieces interact with one another through the Strengths Liberation Statement.

They are:

1. Your dominant domain(s)
2. Your #5 Strength
3. Your #1 Strength
4. Your #34 Strength

We're going to take those four pieces and create a Strengths Liberation Statement that can immediately help you lock into who you are and where your energy is highest, while acknowledging and then dismissing those things that are inauthentic to you.

Here is the template for a Strengths Liberation Statement:

I love to

(the thing you want)_____

in a way that honors my desire to

(dominant desire)_____

and

(secondary desire) _____.

I don't have to worry about being

(#34 Strength description)_____

or

(something else about #34)_____.

Instead I get to be

(#5 Description) _____

and

(#1 Description) _____.

Let me show you how mine looks.

"I love to help the world love itself in a way that honors my desire to move people forward and to think, create, and learn. I don't have to worry about creating consensus and making sure that everyone is on the same page. Instead I get to follow the inner compass of my heart, follow my instincts, and then choose the best way to move myself, my family, my team, and my clients forward."

My statement reflects my dominant desires as an Influencer/Strategic Thinker, my #34 - Harmony®, my #5 - Self Assurance®, and my #1 - Strategic®
My wife's strengths liberation statement looks like this:

"Angela loves to build her business in a way that honors her desire to move people forward and make sure things are done the right way. She doesn't have to worry about deepening her own knowledge base through study and research. Instead she gets to take all the tasks, information, and people around her, find the right place where they fit, and then work towards taking herself, her team, and her people to the next level of performance."

Her statement reflects her desire as an Influencer/Executor, her #34 - Learner®, her #5 - Arranger® and her #1 - Maximizer®.

This is the Strengths Liberation Statement for my business associate, Steve.

"Steve loves to build the Unleash Your Strengths movement in a way that honors his desire to connect with the right people and think and create. He doesn't have to worry about doing it all by himself, by being a go-getter, and setting the pace of production. Instead he gets to decide who the best people are to connect with to grow the business and partner with them using his upbeat personality and contagious enthusiasm for the cause."

His statement reflects his desire as a Relationship Builder/Strategic Thinker, his #34 - Achiever®, his #5 - Strategic®, and his #1 - Positivity®.

Here's the liberation statement for Steve's wife, one of my coaches and friends.

"Jenny loves to coach her clients in a way that honors her desire to connect with the right people. She doesn't have to worry about coming up with the best business building strategy. Instead, she gets to surround herself with people who have potential, connect with them through feeling their feelings, and then coach people who want to move to the next level."

Her statement reflects her desire as a Relationship Builder, her #34 - Strategic®, her #5- Developer®, her #1 - Empathy® and her #2 -

Maximizer®.

I could go on and on, sharing the Strengths Liberation Statements of some of my other coaches, my Customer Experience Manager, my Executive Assistant, my children, and my friends. With each statement I feel a sense of gratitude for who these wonderful people are and see how they get to let go of their bottom strengths as we work together. It's ok that Angela isn't highly energized by deep study and research. She gets to learn in a way that is more experiential, arrange all the people and tasks, and then lead her team to their greatest potential. It's ok that Steve isn't a massive go-getter who burns the candle at both ends, he's great at developing relationships with the right people to grow our business. It's ok that Jenny isn't highly energized by thinking strategically about all the ways to build her coaching business, she just gets to see the potential in other people, feel their emotions and help them reach their potential with her strengths.

It's your turn. It's your turn to not only see how you get to use your strengths, but also how the people around you get to use their strengths. It's powerful and it's liberating. It frees your mind to focus on the right information. It frees you to focus on the right people to connect with and move forward. It frees you to do everything your way. Best of all, it gives you permission to do it all at a higher level.

One more thing to conclude this chapter. I've given you FOUR pieces of your strengths report that give you an amazing distillation of who you are. Once you dig into this work though, you'll see how you can let go of your other bottom strengths. You'll see how your top strengths add all these wrinkles and nuances to who you are. If you're in the business of helping other people, managing teams, or leading organizations, you'll be able to see how you can work effectively with anyone, no matter their strengths, just by helping them do the things that move your organization forward their way.

QUESTIONS:

HOW DOES YOUR STRENGTHS LIBERATION STATEMENT MAKE YOU FEEL?

WHAT DO YOU FEEL MORE EQUIPPED TO DO WITH THIS INFORMATION?

CHAPTER 16
DO EVERYTHING YOUR WAY

I'm going to break down four different categories that I want you to focus your strengths on in the next chapter. We're going to get clear about where you are in four different areas, and then we're going to talk about how you can apply your strengths to everything, your way.

These four categories are:
1. Your Health
2. Your Relationships
3. Your Belief in Yourself
4. Your Business, Job, or Income.

Health can include multiple areas from emotional, mental, and physical well being, but we're going to simplify it by focusing on two things: 1. how your body moves and 2. what you feed it. When we're trying to pick foods or nutrition, or even the information you intake, how are you choosing those things? Are you choosing them with your bottom strengths, or your top strengths? When it comes to moving your body, are you choosing to do things physically in a way that honors your top strengths, or your bottom ones? I'll explain how to do them your way momentarily, but first, I want you to measure where you're starting from. On a scale of one (Struggling) to five (Excellent), where would you rate your health?

Struggling   1   2   3   4   5   Excellent

The second category we're going to talk about is your relationship with you, and with the people around you, in that order. What we want to ask ourselves is how to improve those relationships, and it's simply this: time. We give time to the people that matter most, starting with your spiritual guide. For me, it's God. Then there's the relationship with yourself. How do you treat and talk to yourself? How do you treat everyone else around you? To improve those relationships, it means to add more time. How do you make sure that you are creating more time for relationships that matter, and are they built in your top strengths?

Struggling   1   2   3   4   5   Excellent

Now, your belief in you is not about your spiritual, emotional or psychological health. It has more to do with your belief in your abilities and your potential. In order to develop a belief in your abilities and your potential, you must spend time giving yourself credit for the things you do well so that you can continuously do them. Where are you on a scale of one to five? (but make sure you give yourself credit for the things you do well). Once you decide the number, ask yourself if you are doing this in your top strengths, or your bottom strengths.

Struggling   1   2   3   4   5   Excellent

Your business is the final category. This could also be your income or job. I only want you to think about two parts. One: what you're doing to generate an income, and two: what you're doing to improve your skills to generate an income. Where do you rank yourself on the scale in both of these parts? A score of 1 would mean you are not developing yourself and not generating an income. Five would be constantly generating an income and developing yourself daily.

Struggling   1   2   3   4   5   Excellent

When you're looking at these four different categories and you're seeing these scores, I want you to consider the best way to improve these scores is to lean on your top strengths. Look at the simple activities required to grow these areas. My favorite analogy is the elevator analogy. If you were invited to an event on the 10th floor in a hotel, it doesn't matter what your strengths are. You're still going to have to go to the elevator, hit the button for the doors to open, get in the elevator, and then hit the button for the 10th floor. The doors close and you go to the 10th floor. We all have to do those basic things, but for some of us, when we get to the elevator, we add extra steps or rules. Maybe we only get in an elevator by ourselves, or with certain numbers of people in it. Maybe we press the button to hold the door open or hit the other button to close it as quickly as possible. Some of us just take the stairs. My point in this analogy is that we all have to do the basic things to get success. In any of these four categories, once you know what the basic things are, you can bring your own style and flair to do it your way.

My favorite example, when it comes to exercise, is that if you're going to exercise and you are a dominant Relationship Builder or an Influencer, the best way to do it is around other people where you're constantly encouraging or pushing other people. If you're a dominant Executor, the best way to exercise is to do things systematically: building from the small to the big, keeping it small and consistent is going to be the best way to honor your strengths through the whole process.

As a Strategic Thinker, the best way to exercise is to use this process as a learning tool, to help you learn about how the body works, how your body works, or to learn about something while you exercise. This is an intellectually stimulating process to see what you're learning. When it comes to exercise, eating foods that are high in nutritious value is best done for Relationship Builders and Influencers when they're done in a way that involves other people, either doing it with them, or teaching others. My wife and I both hate cooking, but if you turn on a camera, because we are both dominant Influencers, then we're going to cook like Chef Gordon Ramsay. Why? Because we're cooking in a way that honors both of our desires to move people forward, so we want to be encouraging. That's my point!

When it comes to relationships, understand that all of us know how to connect with people, but we connect with them in our own way. If you're a dominant Relationship Builder or Influencer, you understand that spending time with the people that you want to connect with is the easiest thing to do. It's what energizes you. If you're a dominant Executor, however, you may want to productively connect with the right people by getting something done in the process or having an outcome or a result from the connection time. So, as a dominant Executor, you do the best relationship building when you're building relationships with people who have the same desires for productivity, as you do.

With strategic thinking, it's really quite simple. If you're a dominant Strategic Thinker and you have a love for books, seminars, podcasts or webinars, then start seeing the people that you want to connect with as interesting sources of information, just like you see all of those trainings that you listen to. People are endlessly fascinating. When you start to see people in their strengths, no matter how they show up, it's interesting to learn more about them. That's how you build better relationships to build belief in yourself.

The simple actions required to make progress in any area of your life is to do those things in your strengths. Take note of the success that you have and then replicate it. Believe that being who you are is always going to work.

How do you do that as an Influencer and Relationship Builder? Let it show through the people you are connecting with and moving forward. One of my favorite things to teach Influencers is this quote, "Let the worlds you impact, show you how you impact the world." As a Relationship Builder, it's the exact same when it comes to whom you're connecting with.

Your belief in yourself is built on how you connect and move other people forward. It's powerful when you realize that just being who you are helps other people. As an Executor, it's easy to build the belief in yourself, because you can see how you spend so much of your time measuring your productivity. When you go to bed at night, you see how productive you are. What's important as an Executor to remember is that you can measure anything, even connecting with people. As a Strategic Thinker, the best way to build belief in yourself is to use your strengths as a way of understanding and learning more about you. The more you learn about you and the more you learn about the value you bring to others, and the world, the more you realize that being who you are always works, especially when you're using your mind.

Now, the last one, which is business, is very simple. We're talking about using information to improve our skills, and then applying that information to build and develop our ability to make more money. When you're a Relationship Builder or an Influencer, try to see the best ways to improve your income through connection and moving people forward. Influencers, especially, can make a fortune by helping other people get from where they are, to where they want to be. Relationship Builders can do the same thing through the connection by saying, "We're going to do this together." An Influencer would say, "I'm going to help you get from where you are to where you want to be." When it comes to being an Executor, it's focusing on processes and giving them a dollar value. You can see all the things you do step by step.

For example, if you have Discipline® high you can actually measure how productive things are by looking at the income you're generating and saving by yourself. "The processes that I currently use generate X amount of dollars. In order to exponentially grow those dollars, I have to shift the way I produce or the way I do things on a consistent basis." That can involve bringing other people in to be a part of that process, or doing research on how other people's processes bring in and generate income for them.

Strategic Thinkers do best to improve their income by using their knowledge and leveraging the value of that knowledge. Most people don't want to spend time reading books or going through blogs or listening to podcasts, unless they are also Strategic Thinkers. That means that your natural desire to gather information is valuable in its own rights. So, you can actually generate an income or even a business, based on your ability to gather and organize information, to help other people get to those processes faster. Look at how your ability to use your mind helps you improve your skills at your job.

This whole picture that I'm trying to paint for you is to help you look for ways you can do the basic, structured activities required to improve all these different areas of your life, your way, once you nail down what those basic activities are.

Let's look at how to lay out targets so you can get a bit more clear about what it is you really want to create for yourself, and then bring in your Strengths Proclamation and your Strengths DNA to make it happen in a way that is energizing to you.

QUESTION:

**WHAT'S THE ONE AREA OF YOUR LIFE THAT YOU WOULD MOST
LIKE TO FOCUS ON IN YOUR STRENGTHS?**

CHAPTER 17
GOAL SETTING

Oh boy. How did you feel when you saw the title of this chapter? My bet is that most people will skip this chapter completely.

There's a fascinating connection between the Relationship Builders and goal setting that I have discovered. I'll mention it briefly, but I don't want them to feel like I'm picking on them. It's just something I noticed. Relationship Builders often hate the term "goal setting" because they believe it means "promise making." What I've learned is that if we're not clear about what we truly want for ourselves, more often than not, we're not really going to get it. Think about that for just a moment. There is something that we all want. Most of us are unclear about what that is, and when we're unclear about it, it doesn't make the desire go away. We still have the desire, but because we are unclear about it, we're not getting it.

Relationship Builders tend to want to accomplish goals organically, which means it just happens accidentally in some way, shape, or form. They just want to make it about other people. Thus, goal setting is like making it all about themselves; the opposite of what they truly want.

Now, the truth is that Relationship Builders aren't the only ones that see goal setting this way. No matter what your domain is, do you look at goal setting as a promise, and does it deflate you? That is why I want to talk about goal setting so much. I want to clarify that it is not making promises. It's about laying out targets. I want you to imagine you're going out into a field with a bow and a quiver full of arrows. Where are we going to fire these arrows? Where are you going to stand? Where are you going to aim? How will you know if you are improving your ability to shoot arrows? The only way to do this is to have a target laid out in front of you. A target simply gives you a direction to aim your arrow.

The way I look at goal setting is walking up to a target and having unlimited arrows in my quiver. I hope that eases your mind. It is vitally important to understand this concept. It's why we're here. It's the purpose of applying your strengths: to get what you want and to get it in a way that honors who you are.

There are three questions that you're going to answer during this chapter to help you get clear about what it is you really want, and then we're going to bring your strengths into the conversation. Eric Worre introduced this concept to me. He is one of the top network marketing coaches in the world. He is incredible. I've watched him many times, and I've seen his live events. I'm going to give my interpretation of what he said, but 99% of this is all his, and I love it too much to not share. He explained that there are three types of goal setters.

First is the pessimist. I can guarantee that if you're reading this, you are not a pessimist, because a true pessimist would never go through a book on strengths. They definitely would never go to a chapter on goal setting. They would disregard it completely. So, although you're not a pessimist, we need to understand who the pessimists are to understand the other two types more clearly. A pessimist does not set goals. They will say negative things as-suming the worst all the time. I used to say, "if it goes well, I'll be grateful, and then expect it to go bad again." Pessimists prefer not to set goals at all, and not set any intentions towards anything. They'd rather just live and assume we're going to die, and there's nothing afterwards. The bottom line for me is that a pessimist is not someone I can work with, because they have no interest in moving forward. There's nothing here for you.

The second is the realist, which is predominantly found through-out the world. Somewhere between 80 and 85% of the population refers to themselves as "realists." They set a goal based on what they know they can do. Now here's the funny part. I want you to raise your hand. I'm going to raise my hand, and anybody reading this, raise your hand as well. Look at yourself in the mirror or look at your hand being up in the air. I want you to realize that the peo-ple whose hands are up are the people who suck at knowing what they're capable of. So, what do they do? They set a goal based on what they believe they're capable of. So, if we're looking at poten-tial between one and ten, a realist will set their intention at about five. Now, remember, realists most often prefer to set their goals tial between one and ten, a realist will set their intention at about five. Now, remember, realists most often prefer to set their goals cautiously, because they can do it. In their heads, just as it is with Relationship Builders, that goal is a promise.

If they don't hit that goal, then they've been a disappointment to themselves and other people. They set the goal based on a realistic number. In this case, we'll say five. They'll work and work from one to two to three, and then they'll hit four and fall short. They get upset and feel like they've done something wrong. They have a negative reaction to not achieving their goal, and when they set their next goal, be it the next day, week, month, or year they will reduce their expectation from five to four, based on their perceived failure. They will go back to work again, but only after a period of hesitation between missing the first goal and creating a new one.

There was defeat, depression, a lot of anger, frustration, and a whole lot of moving backward. When they finally get the guts up to set a new goal, it is lowered. They will work and work, fall short again, and repeat the entire process until their goal goes from five, to four, down to three, and continue diminishing. They eventually become pessimists and stop setting goals. I hope you can see this all written out, and understand how this systematic depreciation of your goals can be devastating.

The third type of goal setter is a Visionary. The visionary sets their goal at about a hundred. So, our pessimist is at zero, our realist is quickly backpedaling from five downward, and our visionary is starting their goal at 100. Here's the funny thing about the visionary. They set some crazy, over exuberant goal that is totally based on emotion, excitement, and inspiration, or whatever has driven them to action. They set that goal at 100, and they work to get to four, and then five, and then they get to 20. Twenty is really short of their goal, and just like everyone else, they get frustrated and beat themselves up as well. But, their goal of 100 stays the same. It doesn't falter. They try again, and this time, they work really hard and get somewhere around 23. "Dang it!" they say. They get angry, look at their drawing board, question their thoughts and goals, "I don't know, but it's there, and I have got to hit it! I have to achieve it. This means something to me. Let's try again!" Their goal is still there, and they will continue to fight for it.

Do you see what happened? In their quest for 100 they clearly went beyond the realist and the pessimist. Sure, maybe they only got to 23 (so far), but it's way beyond what they would have achieved had their goals been more "realistic."

So what do you want to be? Clearly not the pessimist, right? The realist isn't much better because you will constantly underestimate your value, think you know what you're capable of, and constantly depreciate your production. Or do you want to just release the idea that your goals are promises and be a visionary who is committed to finding out who they can truly be? How do you want to set your goals? For me, my friends, I have this crazy goal. I have this goal to get in a million people to my private strengths group. That's insane! I don't even know how to get in front of a million people, let alone have a million people choose to buy into my group. You see, in order for me to get a million people to buy into my group, I have to present my group to about one hundred million people. That's about where I'm aiming at right now.

Yea, okay, maybe 10 million would be sufficient, and maybe 100 million is too much? How do I get in front of 10 million people? There are people that know how to do it, I'm sure of that, but I'm not one of them, yet. It's an insane goal, but why does it matter to me? That's the whole point. When I look at this insane goal of a million people joining my group, I'm not making a promise to you or me or anybody. I'm just setting out a target and I'm going to do what I can to make it happen. Why? Because I'm out to prove it, because I can't sit here and believe that I'm the only person that has this idea. That would make me feel like I'm doing something wrong.

As of the second edition of this book, I have over 1,500 people in the group. There was no way I would have seen that happen, had I not set this crazy high goal! There is no way I would ever say to myself that I am capable of getting 1,500 people into my private group, yet I did it. It happened. So, while I don't yet know how to get to 1,000,000 people, I'm going to work to find out how far I can truly expand. I set a crazy, insane goal, but I'm clear about why it matters to me, and I'm going after it. That's the whole point I want to make here. I want you to decide right now, which one of these three kinds of goal setters are you going to be?

What is it that you want? What is it that you care about? What is something that matters to you? What. Do. You. Want? I learned the importance of this question a long time ago, when someone asked me. I hated who I was, so I had no idea what I wanted, but when they asked me and refused to let me off the hook, I had to answer it. It forced me to get clear about what it is I want. Most of us go through our whole lives assuming that it's bad to have something that we want, as if it's bad to be a little selfish, to be clear about what matters most to us. Because of that, most of us worry about what other people want, which we already discussed is a bad idea, when we talked about the three businesses earlier.

In order to stay in our strengths, we have to get clear about what it is we want. So, what do you want? There are a couple of rules. Do not give me a general answer like, "I want to believe in myself," or "I want financial freedom." I want you to tell me what you want, something measurable that you can show me when you get it. Don't try to be inspiring.

I also get this type of answer a lot, "I want to open up schools for children with autism so that I can change the way students are being taught." Honestly, that's wonderful, but what does it have to do with you? What do you want? What do you care about? What is the most important thing for you to focus on indefinitely? What do you want? If someone tells me they want time and freedom, I press further. What does that look like? If you want financial freedom, great, but how much money do you need to have that freedom? How much more money do you want? More time? How much more time do you want to believe in yourself? What would you be able to do if you believed in yourself? Do you want a powerful marriage, a powerful relationship with your kids, and a powerful relationship with yourself? What does that look like? Be clear with what you want.

What do you want? _____
_____
_____.

The second question gets a little emotional and I want you to be comfortable with the fact that it's okay to feel emotions. So, why does it matter to you if you get it? Why do you care? If you get it, how would you feel versus how you feel right now? Why does it matter to you if you get it?

I remember the first time someone asked me this. My brain just snapped, and I said, "I want a million dollars in my bank account." That's extremely uninspiring. There is nothing about that that makes other people go, "ooh, I want to know more." But, that's because you don't know why. So, when I blurted out that answer, my wife looked at me in shock, because her husband, who had just spent the last five years hating himself, finally wanted something. She cried when she heard me tell her what I wanted, because the second part, which is why it matters to me, was the most important part at the time. It's because I wanted to believe in myself. If I could figure out how to generate a million dollars into my bank account, then I could finally feel like I'm valuable. That's why it mattered to me. That's why I cared. It wasn't about the money, but being able to measure value with it. One of my favorite mentors, Jim Rohn, said, "Make one of your goals to be a millionaire so that you could just give that money away because who you became was far more valuable." Ooh, I love that so much!

He was right. I made it my mission to figure out how to create value, to put a million dollars into my bank account, so that I could look at people and prove my value. The good news is I discovered that I don't need a million dollars to be valuable, but my mission still stayed the same: I am here to make an impact on a lot of people, and that matters because I need to believe that I'm valuable. That's what pushes me to do more.

Why does your goal matter to you? _____
_____
_____
_____
_____
_____.

The last question, my friends, is definitely the most important one, because this is the one to get you moving. There will be times in your life, while you push towards the thing that you want,, where you will be challenged. You will experience fear, stress, and resistance to vulnerability. You're going to see other people around who doubt you. All kinds of things are going to come at you to stop you from doing the things that you want to do, that you need to do, to get what you want. If you don't have the answer to this question,

then you're going to give up, just like I did over and over and over again.

What is going to happen if you never do what you need to do to get what you want? I use the word, "never" on purpose, because a lot of time people will try to answer with their Positivity® strength, "I'll just keep working until I get it!" No. You didn't hear the question. What happens if you NEVER do what you need to do to get the thing you want? What happens next?

Most of us go through life never fully dealing with the consequences of a lack of action. We just think that if we put it off, we'll try again tomorrow. "Try again tomorrow" becomes our mantra, and today we never do. One of my favorite comedians, Dimitri Martin, said this, and it made me laugh so hard, "I love starting weight loss programs. I'm not very good at finishing them. So, I have this collection of photos of me naked and sad, just a bunch of photos of me looking naked and sad because I never finished the programs." Hilarious!

I want you to imagine your life this way, where you never finish the program, because you keep saying, "I'll try again tomorrow."

What is going to happen if you never do what you need to do to get what you want? _____
_____
_____
_____
_____
_____.

If you can answer this question and get clear about the consequences of not moving forward, then we can move into your strengths because I want you to think about this thing that you want as the thing we're going to focus on moving forward. What I want you to do is go back to that thing that you want, that you wrote down, whether it's monetary, a weight loss goal, a successful marriage, or any other want. Whatever it is, write it down somewhere that you will see each day.

Now, I want you to add that to your Strengths Proclamation and say, " I love to _____ _____ (insert the thing that you want) in a way that honors my desire to _____ _____ and _____.

I love to have a million dollars in my bank account in a way that honors my desire to move people forward and think, create, and learn.

Now, go into your Strengths DNA and start with your #5 strength, then go to your #1 and then boom, boom, boom with the rest of the DNA.

Do you understand what I'm saying? You're now looking at what you want. You're clear about why it matters, and you're clear about the consequences of not doing what you need to do to get it.

With that heavy emphasis on it, write out your goal using your Strengths Proclamation and your Strengths DNA. Then post it somewhere visible for you to see it.

CHAPTER 18
BECOME A LEADER YOUR WAY

One of my favorite things about Gallup® is their ability to poll the world. Honestly, if I had that kind of access, I might be able to achieve my goal of a million people in about a week.

One of the things they did was poll millions of people and ask them, what is it that you look for in a leader? They asked for people to give them the qualities of leaders that they follow. Gallup® did the research, and after millions and millions of responses. They narrowed down the top four qualities that everyone's looking for in a leader.

What I want you to do as I'm going through these four different qualities is think about how you can exemplify those qualities your way, as a Relationship Builder, Executor, Strategic Thinker, or Influencer, no matter your unique combination of strengths. Apply your dominant domain and your strengths in a way that honors these qualities, so that other people can follow you. The important thing to remember is that you get to exemplify leadership your way.

The four qualities are trust, hope, compassion, and stability. These are the four qualities that millions and millions of people have determined, this is what they're looking for in people they want to follow. As a leader, it means that you're going to encourage other people to move forward with you. Even if it's helping them move forward in their own way. If you commit to exemplifying these qualities at your highest level with your top strengths, then your ability to influence others becomes exponentially easier.

I'm going to break down these four qualities, lay out the steps, and explain how you can, with your strengths, do it your way.

TRUST

I love trust, because it's so simple. The way to prove to another person that you are someone who is trustworthy, is to consciously do everything with the intention to prove to them that all you want to do is help. Think about subtext this way. Imagine that everything that came out of your mouth was, you really saying, "All I want to do is help you." Imagine if you went up to people who you wanted to help and told them, "All I want to do is help." The best way for us to create trust is to always be doing things in a way that authentically brings value to other people.

I am obsessed with being of value to you. All I want to do is help. I know how to apply my strengths. I know all the secrets. I know things that even the most talented Gallup® strengths coaches do not know. I am happy with my knowledge. I don't have to share it with you. Except that, I want to do that through this book. If you believe me, then I have done my job to prove to you that I am someone who is trustworthy.

What I want you to do is think about how you can do this as a Relationship Builder. The best way for a Relationship Builder to build trust is to connect with people with no agenda.

As an Influencer, the best way to create trust is to let people know that all you want to do is help them establish what they want, and then be of value.

The best way for Executors to create trust is to let them know how good you are at making sure things are done the right way. All you want to do is apply those talents to help them get what they want.

As a Strategic Thinker, all you have to do is let them know how your information and knowledge has helped you and all you want to do is use it to help them.

To create trust you must communicate with everything you do that all you want to do is help. That's it. It's that simple.

HOPE

The second quality of a leader is hope. Help other people see that they can get from where they are to where they want to be. The most effective way to do that is to share your story. You see, if you want to help other people move past their blocks, paint a picture of where you were, the epiphanies you had, the obstacles you overcame, and how you (and they) can get the thing that they desperately want. Help them see that it's possible.

In order to create hope, you must stop and give yourself credit for overcoming your own problems, overcoming your own blocks, overcoming your own difficulties and overcoming your own fears. So you share your story about where you were before. Where and how you were introduced to the thing that helps you overcome these issues. Share how you feel now about yourself.

When it comes to strengths, it's easy for me. I shared with you how much I struggled in my life before I was introduced to strengths. I shared with you how I learned about strengths so that you can understand that I didn't embrace it right away. But I gave it a chance. And then I let you know the payoff, how it's helped me, how it has changed my life, how it has helped me help thousands of others. Sharing my story creates hope for you.

It is my hope that you've been able to see that you can make those transitions your way. You can share your story and create hope for others. Be vulnerable. Embrace your journey and share it with other people.

As a Relationship Builder you're creating hope by connecting with the right people. As an Influencer you're doing that to help people move from where they are to where they want to be. As an Executor you're doing it to be productive for you and them. As a Strategic Thinker you're creating hope for others by sharing your knowledge and expertise.

COMPASSION

The reason why I share it in this order is because I want you to understand hope first, so that the compassion becomes so simple. The way that you show compassion for other people, is you give them a break for being where you once were. Letting them know, "It's okay," and saying to yourself, "these people are doing the best they can with everything that they know." You and I, and the rest of the world are so good at judging other people for the silly things they do. What I want you to do is realize you're not judging them. You're judging you. I's time to give you and them a break.

Have some compassion. Be willing to let people know that it's okay for them to be where they are. Because they're doing their best with what they know. At this point, you can invite them. Do you want more, because I would love to just help. I've been there before. And I've done that. And I've made a transition.

You see what's wonderful about focusing on compassion third is because you can see how leading with, "Hey I'm just here to help" (trust) then, "I've been where you are," helps you to give compassion towards other people. Compassion is powerful. Because the thing that will get in your way of helping others, is to beat them up for being where they are. Stop beating people up for where they are. Give them a break. They're doing the best they can with what they know and then ask them, "Do they want support, do they want encouragement, do they want your help? Do they want more?" If they do, be trustworthy and give them hope.

STABILITY

The last one, Stability, is the most important to me. And it's the simplest to do, but it's the one we all want to resist. To give stability is simply showing up for others. A lot of us are getting into our heads, about how we need to show up. We think we need to show up perfectly. We all think we need to show up flawlessly and with all the answers. We believe the best way to show up is to be perfect before we can show up for someone else.

I'm telling you right now friends, that is not showing up at all. Showing up is simply showing up. That's it. So if somebody needs you to show up in your pajamas, with your hair undone, not knowing anything. Just show up. Just be there.

I know a lot of you are probably going to be triggered when I say this, but it's really about consistency over quality. All the things I've done that have helped me market myself have been a commitment to consistency over quality. Heck, the first version of this book was chock full of grammatical errors, misspelled words, and even a big mistake on the cover. I was committed to getting it done and getting it out there. One thousand people said, "It doesn't have to be perfect Eddie. Thanks for showing up with this inspiring message."

Quality comes over time when consistency comes first.

When I first began marketing myself I did videos every day for years. The first two years of videos that I did, I can't even look at them anymore. They are awful. Right now I'm in my seventh year of doing online marketing. I can't even stomach watching those old videos. They're such poor quality. But the fact that I did them consistently is what generated value for other people. I showed up. I have done thousands of videos and hundreds of training modules and webinars. I never stopped showing up.

The things I talked about five years ago are not the things I talk about now. In fact, some of the things I talked about five years ago are actually wrong. I've actually made some mistakes. I actually said things that I thought were true that turned out to not be true. The bottom line is, I showed up. And that's what I want you to think about for yourself.

Have you shown up?

That's it. All you have to do is show up.

So how does a Relationship Builder show up? You pick up the phone and you connect, with no agenda. Just pick up the phone and connect with somebody. You can even send a voice message to the people that you care about.

An Influencer can show up by being there for others and sharing value. You can teach and inspire through video trainings, webinars, blogs, and podcasts. Just do them consistently.

An Executor can show up by being someone dependable and letting people know you are available to help them get things done the right way.

As a Strategic Thinker, show up with your knowledge and share it with other people. Strategic Thinkers are amazing at collecting information and then creating content. It's so simple. Create content and post it every single day and let the people decide what pieces of content matter to them and what doesn't. Watch how your consistent sharing of information makes you a trusted source for hundreds and then thousands of people.

Ultimately, when you exemplify all four of these qualities, you become a leader your way and make it easy for other people to follow you. Imagine yourself as a broadcast radio station. All you're doing all day long is broadcasting: "Trust me. All I want to do is help you. I failed and I have succeeded. I'm giving you a break for being where you are and I will always be here."

Always be broadcasting those messages, use your strengths to share your messages, and the people that you want to attract will show up.

I hope you enjoyed that. We're gonna move on to the next subject, which is how do you show up consistently without getting overwhelmed.

QUESTIONS:

HOW DO YOU EXEMPLIFY HOPE, TRUST, STABILITY & COMPAS-
SION?

CHAPTER 19
TIME TO MOVE

One of the biggest takeaways from the last chapter was hopefully the stability part: doing things consistently and always being there. A lot of us get overwhelmed at the idea of doing things every single day, but that is what I'm challenging you to do. Do things for your health every single day. Do things for your relationships every single day. Do things for your belief in yourself every single day. Do things for your income every single day. Don't take days off. Simplify your big dream so you can be consistent every day instead of making it too big and overwhelming.

We have chosen to believe that in order to have success, we need to have home runs. We're going to get into some baseball analogies, my friends. Hopefully you understand enough about it to know what the heck I'm talking about here.

I want you to picture a guy on a baseball field. The game just began and he's thinking to himself, "okay, I've got two options here. I can knock the ball over the fence or I can get a base hit."

We all love home runs, don't we? Why? Because you take that bat, and with one swing, you send that ball flying over the wall and everyone cheers. Home runs are sexy. Home runs get right to the point with one swing of the bat. The batter gets to trot around the bases, and flip the bat to make the other team angry. It's show off time. They got one point with one swing. But let's be honest. Home runs aren't easy. Obviously they're difficult, or we wouldn't cheer so loudly for them!

So the batter could swing for the fences, get the home run and get one point. Or he can knock the ball out of the infield and get a base hit. Typically, these base hits are accompanied by a polite golf clap from the crowd, instead of a roaring screams from smashing it all the way to the moon.

The reason we don't get as excited about base hits is because they're not worth a point on their own. However, base hits are setting up more productivity. A base hit on its own simply sets another batter up to continue moving the first hitter forward to the next base.

A lot of us in our lives do base hits all the time, but we don't give ourselves any credit for it because it's not as exciting and sexy as a home run. However, I want you to consider what happens if the next batter comes up and does the same thing. Now you have two on base, continuing on with the next batter. The next batter could hit a home run and get their team three points, but home runs are still difficult. Instead, keep filling those bases and doing base hits so that each player moves forward, and the points keep building. You keep things simple and easy, and you keep getting points.

Basically, four easy base hits are worth the same as one home run. So, what happens if you have another person come up and do another base hit? You continue scoring points. Now that the bases are continually loaded, scoring points becomes easier and easier. Every time a new player gets a base hit, points get scored consistently.

Are you getting excited about this? What I'm telling you is how to get big home run results by doing simple actions. I want you to realize that consistency is what creates quality. What happens if a batter comes up and says, "Well, I'm going to do something great. I'm going to hit a grand slam and send all bases home, scoring us four points." What happens when they strike out? Three productive base hits are "left on base." What if another batter comes up with the intent to show off the big swing and drive them all home, yet strikes out? The baserunners get left on base again, until the inning ends, the runners go back to the dugout, and the team has to start all over again.

It's so much more productive if we just keep things small, but consistent. Let's give you some examples. First, improving your health. Instead of changing your whole diet, you just change breakfast for a week. That's it. You can still eat like crap for lunch and dinner, but your breakfast is going to be healthy and planned. Great! There's your base hit. After a couple of weeks, you step it up and start eating a healthy breakfast and lunch. Instead of going from no exercise to trying to run a marathon, take a walk first. Condition your body and spend 30 minutes each day walking, until you feel comfortable enough to make it a longer time, or more intense. You add in jogging and running once you've built up that stamina to be able to do so.

In relationships, try talking to a couple people each day that you'd like to connect with once a week. In your business, instead of trying to figure out how to market your business by hiring a $50,000 coach, get some free programs and learn from there. As you earn income from what you've learned for free, invest in an inexpensive program. Earn income from the inexpensive program and then invest in the more expensive program that can help you grow and give you opportunities and skills.

When I was first building my business, I started by watching free trainings. I would take those free trainings and invest them into my work to generate an income, even if it was $20 or $30. I would turn around and reinvest that into more expensive programs, until I ended up purchasing a $3,500 program. It had all the software and accessories with it. Today, it's generated hundreds of thousands of dollars for me, but I started off small.

Lastly, I want to talk about building your belief in you and the "Success Formula" for achieving it. Look at this formula with the context of base hits in mind. Remember the whole point is to make everything you do smaller, so you can continue the consistency every day, because it creates quality.

When it comes to the success formula of applying your strengths to your belief in self, it starts off like this:

1. Take your unique talents and strengths. Remember, you are infinitely unique and cannot be duplicated.

2. Use your top 10 strengths for your Strengths Proclamation and your Strengths DNA. It's you. Nobody else has the same combination.

3. Action. You take your strengths and put them to work. There is going to be a result.

Measure these results by looking at how your strengths came

Measure these results by looking at how your strengths came into play to create value. The formula looks like this: Your unique talents and strengths, plus action, equals results. These results are the small wins, but they keep getting bigger and bigger, until one day you are finally convinced that being you is enough. You are finally there. You're finally letting go of who you aren't, and you're loving and embracing who you are, simply through the collection of small base hit activities that you do every day.

The point in all of this is to stop hesitating because your dreams are so big. Stop swinging for the fences. Take your big dreams and break them down into small pieces that can grow each day and build off one another. This should make it very realistic for you. You should be fired up right now, and to be honest, you probably won't want to read the final chapter because you're so ready to work, which is awesome! If you're going to go to work, I ask you to pick one small thing you can do for the next 30 minutes to an hour and just get started. Don't think about the big picture, all the things you need to do. Think of the smallest one, write it down, and go do that one thing in a way that honors your Strengths Proclamation and your Strengths DNA. You mapped it now, now have fun making it happen.

WHAT ARE THE BASE HITS YOU CAN DO EVERY DAY TO IM-
PROVE YOUR:

HEALTH

BUSINESS

RELATIONSHIPS

BELIEF IN YOURSELF

HOW DOES "SWINGING FOR THE FENCES" CAUSE YOU TO
STRIKE OUT?

CHAPTER 20
THE FINAL TAKEAWAYS

All right, my friends, we have gone through this entire book and I just want to sum up what we've learned so you understand how empowered you are right now.

When we first started off, we learned about the whole point of strengths, and what makes them awesome, which is really about what makes you awesome. I walked you through things I've come to learn about the value of strengths, which is how I learned to see my true value. My hope is that you have been seeing your own journey in that process.

We talked about the domains. You figured out who you really are, and what must be honored with everything you do.

You learned your Strengths Proclamation, where you get to share who you are, and own it.

We talked about your #5 Strength and your #1 Strength and how you can use both of those to honor your dominant domain.

You also learned the power of releasing your bottom strengths, especially your #34, and understanding how they drain you and keep you from your potential and being who you are. Your bottom strengths get in the way of your dominant domain and your #5 and your #1.

We went into the truth about what is amazing about you through your Strengths DNA, your Dominant Natural Actions. It's about being you with everything you do, and following the step by step of your strengths. Remember, start with #5, then #1, then #'s 2,3 & 4 and #'s 6,7,8,9 & 10.

We also recalled how to flip the switch and clarify why our bottom strengths don't work for us. The truth is that being who you are with everything you do is far more productive, and it brings you more joy.

You also learned about how to do everything in your way to improve your health, relationships, income, and belief in self. We talked about the truth in goal setting, and differentiated between target setting and promise making. You understand how to lay out exactly what you want. You get to choose the type of goal setter you want to be, to get clear about what you want, why it matters, and the consequences of not getting it done.

We wrapped up with how to be a leader and make everything small so you can be consistent and create quality.

I want to sum up the final takeaway of this book for me, for my purpose and mission. I have chosen to make Unleash Your Strengths what I do for the rest of my life. This book is one of many that I will be doing over the next several years. There will be books and audiobooks on how to unleash your strengths on every aspect of your life that matters to you. Whether you want to use your strengths to be a better investor for finances, or teach, it doesn't really matter, as long as you realize that the best way to do it is your way.

My friends, many of us are conditioned to believe that in order to have what we don't have, we have to be something that we're not. I don't know about you, but I'm sick of it. It's a lie. Being who you are with everything you do will bring everything you want, that you don't currently have. I'm willing to bet that you have learned so much about yourself through this, that you're realizing that being who you are is not who you have been all this time. My hope is that you've made a commitment to figure out exactly who you are or how to be you at the highest level.

Here's what's really wonderful. When you are being you at a very high level, two really magical things happen for the people around you. 1. You make it easy for them to see your value. That's the biggest thing. 2. You make it easy for them to be who they are. How many times have you gone out with friends, and there's always one person who just struggles and makes it uncomfortable for you?

The truth is that when people are struggling with being who they are, or they don't even know who they are, they pretend to be something that they're not. My friends, that is what you do when you doubt yourself, even just for a moment. Whether you're trying to sell something, be a parent, a friend, or whoever, you have to be who you are for the benefit of others. Make it easy for them to see your value and for them to show you who they are.

You see, the truth is that in order for us to be more influential, more productive, more creative, or connect with the right people, we have to do it our way, otherwise we're going to connect with the wrong people. We're going to produce the wrong things. Our creativity is going to suffer. We're going to get in other people's way.

See your value so that other people can too. This book is designed specifically for you to focus on what's great about you and to give you the belief without you having to lie to yourself in the mirror each day. Give up all of that nonsense.

It's time to Unleash Your Strengths!

POSTMARKS

There are lots of resources that I have made available for you and other people. If this book is your introduction to me, there is so much more that I'm creating to make a difference in the world.

Visit www.unleashyourstrengths.com to check out the online community we've created to help thousands of entrepreneurs, network marketers, parents, marriages, and humanitarians come together in a way that honors their desire to take their lives to the next level.

In the community we have a content library plus group coaching calls and live training sessions to help people love and embrace who they are, then achieve results that help their marriage, business, online message, and more. For more information you can email us at assistant@unleashyourstrengths.com.